Million Dollar Influence

Even senior people, business owners, and board members are unaware of the nuances of influence on a daily basis. They think in a straight line and try to "strike deals," use hierarchical power, make "trade-offs," or bargain as if at a flea market.

They unwittingly sacrifice vital needs to gain minor and temporary bright, shiny things. Influence is not about fast-talking, it's about fast-thinking and carefully constructed language that one applies within a specific context. Influence is thought to be programmable—that is, it can create scarcity or consistency of positive responses. In reality, it's about accountability, innovation, and leverage.

No pre-pandemic strategy is worth a cent in a post-pandemic world. There is no "new normal" or "return to normal." There are only new realities. In this book, one of the boldest, most aggressive, most successful consultants in the world makes his predictions and provides recommendations that may frighten and stun, but ultimately can lead to market domination.

Million-dollar influencers understand that influence doesn't mean kissing up to everyone. While we may all be equal as human beings, not everyone has a stake in the outcomes in the business of influence. Some will resist change for the sake of resisting change. They lack imagination or let fear hold them in place. Recognizing actual stakeholders will guide your positioning of stakes in the ground that will mark critical positions leading to your desired outcome.

Features

- How consensus building is something to live with, not something to die for
- The fundamental difference between accountability and authority
- The need for innovation and even improvisation in wielding influence
- The scientific and magical contrasts of language
- How to effectively maneuver within political environments
- How to rally the right stakeholders at the right time
- The powerful role of consequence

Million Dollar Influence

How to Drive Powerful Decisions through Language, Leverage, and Leadership

Alan Weiss

Gene Moran

Routledge
Taylor & Francis Group

A PRODUCTIVITY PRESS BOOK

First published 2023
by Routledge
605 Third Avenue, New York, NY 10158

and by Routledge
Park Square, Milton Park, Abingdon, Oxon, OX14 4RN

Routledge is an imprint of the Taylor & Francis Group, an informa business

ISBN: 978-1-032-34059-3 (hbk)
ISBN: 978-1-032-34061-6 (pbk)
ISBN: 978-1-003-32038-8 (ebk)

DOI: 10.4324/9781003320388

Typeset in Minion pro
by SPi Technologies India Pvt Ltd (Straive)

Contents

Contents vi

About the Authors

Alan Weiss is one of those rare people who can say he is a consultant, speaker, and author and mean it. His consulting firm, Summit Consulting Group, Inc., has attracted clients such as Merck, Hewlett-Packard, GE, Mercedes-Benz, State Street Corporation, Times Mirror Group, The Federal Reserve, The New York Times Corporation, Toyota, and over 500 other leading organizations.

He has served on the boards of directors of the Trinity Repertory Company, a Tony-Award-winning New England regional theater, Festival Ballet, chaired the Newport International Film Festival, and been president of the board of directors of Festival Ballet Providence. His speaking typically includes 20 keynotes a year at major conferences, and he has been a visiting faculty member at Case Western Reserve University, Boston College, Tufts, St. John's, the University of Illinois, the Institute of Management Studies, and the University of Georgia Graduate School of Business. He has held an appointment as adjunct professor in the Graduate School of Business at the University of Rhode Island where he taught courses on advanced management and consulting skills to MBA and PhD candidates.

He once held the record for selling out the highest priced workshop (on entrepreneurialism) in the then-21-year history of New York City's Learning Annex. His Ph.D. is in psychology. He has served on the Board of Governors of Harvard University's Center for Mental Health and the Media. He is an inductee into the Professional Speaking Hall of Fame® and the concurrent recipient of the National Speakers Association Council of Peers Award of Excellence, representing the top 1% of professional speakers in the world. He is a Fellow of the Institute of Management Consultants, one of only two people in history holding both those designations.

His prolific publishing includes over 500 articles and 60 books, including his best-seller, *Million Dollar Consulting* (from McGraw-Hill) now in its 30th year and sixth edition. His newest is *Legacy: Life is not about a search for meaning but the creation of meaning* (Routledge, 2021). His books have been on the curricula at Villanova, Temple University, and the Wharton School of Business, and have been translated into 15 languages.

His career has taken him to 60 countries and 49 states. (He is afraid to go to North Dakota.) Success Magazine cited him in an editorial devoted to his work as "a worldwide expert in executive education." The New York Post called him "one of the most highly regarded independent consultants in America." He is the winner of the prestigious Axiem Award for Excellence in Audio Presentation.

He is the recipient of the Lifetime Achievement Award of the American Press Institute, the first-ever for a non-journalist, and one of only seven awarded in the 65-year history of the association. He holds an annual Thought Leadership Conference which draws world-famous experts as speakers.

He has coached former candidates for Miss Rhode Island/Miss America in interviewing skills. He once appeared on the popular American TV game show Jeopardy, where he lost badly in the first round to a dancing waiter from Iowa. Alan is married to the lovely Maria for 52 years, and they have two children and twin granddaughters. They reside in East Greenwich, RI with their dogs, Coco and Bentley, a white German Shepherd.

Gene Moran is the President of Capitol Integration. He is a strategic advisor to defense and security companies who are selling to the federal government. His strategic influence has resulted in billions of dollars in federal sales for his clients.

His firm, Capitol Integration, is recognized by Bloomberg Government as a Top-Performing Lobbying Firm, and by the National Institute for Lobbying & Ethics where he is designated a "Top Lobbyist." Gene is a Million Dollar Consulting Hall of Fame® inductee and a recipient of the Corrie Shanahan Memorial Award for Advancing Consulting.

Synthesizing his unique experience spanning decades, Gene guides companies through the arcane ways of Washington, DC, integrating his groundbreaking academic research of defense lobbying, deep military experience commanding US Navy ships and advising senior leaders, as well as leadership in corporate government relations. Gene understands and uses influence to educate and inform others while shaping great outcomes.

Introduction

We've written *Million Dollar Influence* because, as two global consultants with corporate and/or military careers that preceded and have informed our current roles, we've experienced a great deal of heat but far from sufficient light in the crucible of influence. People trying to persuade others too often wind up in need of conflict resolution! Too often their mantra is, "Let's compromise and do it my way."

Let's define "influence" for our purposes here in this manner: the power to shape policy or ensure favorable treatment from someone. We regard it as reciprocal, the proverbial "win/win." Yet we're in a competitive age where too often "win/lose" is the dynamic and the sports field carries over to the business field.

In this post-Covid world, *there is neither a "return to normal" nor a "new normal."* However, there are *new realities* which we must embrace and understand. We've learned that accountability and authority are two different aspects of business and life. We've seen how leverage is important and the other person's self-interest is key to our own. And that the dynamics of any "deal" include staying in the moment and applying the rules of improv theater: Never deny, always accept.

Whether your interests in influence are in sales, service, the local town council, a philanthropy, or even family relations, the dynamics are very similar. There is a surfeit of books published annually on the psychological ramifications, the sociological implications, and the political applications. We'll leave all that to the academics.

We're pragmatists. We believe there is an art and science to any "deal" and they are heavily oriented to the establishment of healthy relationships and clear personal methodology and ground rules for mutual success.

Alan has succeeded with this in a global business practice, and Gene has succeeded with this in his practice in federal government relations and stellar military career. Now we want to share these approaches with you to create a successful business and extraordinary life.

— Alan Weiss, PhD, East Greenwich, RI
— Gene Moran, PhD, Bradenton, FL
September 2022

1

Consensus is something you can live with, not something you'd die for

Business executives sometimes make decisions as though they are playing king of the hill, a childhood game. You simply shoved other people or they shoved you.

The speed of information in the continuous news cycle and persistent social media channels convince us that success translates to one winner and an infinite number of losers. This false binary choice clouds our judgment and inhibits the multiple "good enough" solutions that could generate far more sales, allow more partnering opportunities and leave doors open for multiple subsequent sales. Failing to recognize the corrosive nature of our linear thinking will lead to countless missed opportunities.

Million Dollar Influence is about achieving acceptable outcomes, not about dominance.

Influencers

There is almost always more than one way to succeed.

Pareto, an economist, observed that 20% of Italian landowners held 80% of the land. The Pareto Principle has several adaptations over time, becoming the equivalent of the Eleventh Commandment. One such usage recognizes that 80% of the problems come from 20% of the causes. About 80% of revenue in business comes from 20% of clients. The concept applies to global wealth and taxation as well: Twenty percent stand out from the rest for their financial holdings and commensurate tax obligation.

DOI: 10.4324/9781003320388-1

Given the ubiquity of this "80/20" power law principle, it makes sense to consider it in the exercise of influence. But doing so requires that you flip the script. Eighty percent of people spend too much time pursuing the final 20% *that doesn't influence the outcome.* Million Dollar Influencers accept the 80% "good enough" solution and move on to the successive success.

Million Dollar Influence is about moving people through their thinking and decision-making to a preferred outcome. It recognizes that influence is not specifically about "yes or no," right or wrong, good or bad, left or right. Influence does not necessarily require a formulaic prescription to prevail. Merriam-Webster defines consensus as "general agreement." Can we all agree that murder is wrong? That we should drive our cars within reasonable proximity to the speed limit? If we agree to terms of employment, fair pay for honest work should ensue? Each is a form of consensus thinking. They seem reasonable to the overwhelming majority. Some fringe members of any population might disagree with what the overwhelming majority find satisfactory. Let the fringe be what they are: marginal. Million Dollar Influencers see the merit in the use of such broad strokes.

The energy one must expend to find unanimity in most any business or leadership circumstance is orders of magnitude above what will allow necessary progress. Million Dollar Influence recognizes the waste of this additional and fruitless expense. *The juice of getting to 100% agreement is not worth the squeeze.* Good enough can often carry the day. That doesn't mean settling; it means being smart about the cost–benefit.

WHAT PLAYBOOK ARE YOU WORKING FROM?

Some of you are reading this either don't have the correct playbook for your present position or, worse, you don't have one at all. You're coasting on prior learned behaviors. The only way to coast is downhill.

Being "in the moment" is a learnable skill; however, many confuse what amounts to "winging it" with being in the moment. Too often, people underperform in professional settings when they speak in the moment because they don't have an effective plan in mind. What we may think of as being present can appear to our audience as someone thinking aloud as they speak. (Many people do this, and it's called "articulating one's cognitive processes." Or, in layman's terms, listening to something you really can't use.)

Gifted salespeople can convince themselves that they've "got this" when walking into a new sales situation. Occasionally, for those with an uncommon gift, a conversation conveys warmth and friendship while lowering barriers, but it may not advance your desired position or outcome. The concept of hubris dates back to Greek mythology. The term's definition has evolved to include pride, overconfidence, and arrogance. Don't confuse the outcomes that stem from your hubris with movement toward your preferred outcome.

Influencers

Confidence is the honest-to-God belief you can help others. Arrogance is the sincere belief you have nothing left to learn yourself. Smugness is arrogance without the talent.

As executives and business leaders rise in the ranks, they often rely on academia's communications techniques and interpersonal skills. Think back to your high school "senior superlatives." Can you picture the individuals voted Most Likely to (fill in the blank)? Some displayed natural talents early in life in sports, academics, making friends, public speaking, or election to an office above others. Some moved to the spotlight; others shied away from it. Those good and bad underlying skills, talents, and inclinations may still cloud your perceptions of how well you carry yourself in business. You need a plan.

WHAT IS A WIN?

Our perception of the world is polarized, and we self-select information that reinforces our perceptions. The flow of information is no longer a 24-hour cycle; it is a continuous and unrelenting flow from which we have difficulty stepping back. Mobile phones, communications apps, hundreds of cable and satellite channels, increasing social media options, and our circle of friends and work colleagues bombard us with information. We are overwhelmed with a continuous information flow that we must filter and interpret to make sense of our world. The round-the-clock, hyper-stimulated atmosphere of a Las Vegas casino was once something we could consciously choose to step in or out of.

Our brains need a way to organize information. Confirmation bias is one such mechanism that helps us reinforce beliefs and positions. However, those beliefs can contain emotional anchors rather than rational facts. To simplify our world, we default to a win-lose mindset.

Some examples

Tom Brady is the established GOAT (Greatest of All Time) in the NFL. His leadership of two NFL teams to seven Superbowls is unmatched. During the 2022 playoffs, Brady's Tampa Bay Buccaneers were within four seconds of winning a playoff to compete for an eighth Superbowl. That hope was dashed by a field goal from LA Rams kicker Matt Gay. Game over, and season over for the Buccaneers. Some anticipated accurately that Brady would subsequently retire. There is no consolation prize.

University of Alabama head coach Nick Saban leads the NCAA in coaching seven college football national championships, six of them while at the helm of Alabama. The Southeastern Conference (SEC) is a particularly challenging conference to win so consistently. In 2022, the University of Georgia, which had lost to Alabama during a regular-season game, dominated Alabama to win the national championship. Game over, a new champion is crowned as Georgia wins its first national championship in thirty years. There is no second place, just one champion.

Our political debates in Congress have become a matter of all or nothing. Senators and Members of Congress vote along party lines for most votes. Unless a Senator or Congressperson has a unique situation with a hometown constituency and confers with party leadership about its importance to retaining the seat, members must fall in line and vote with the party. As President Obama, a Democrat, came into office, Senate Minority Leader Mitch McConnell made no secret that his role and ensuing strategy would thwart a Democratic agenda.

As President Trump came to office, Senate Minority Leader Harry Reid, followed by Chuck Schumer, adopted a similar strategy. Recall very high-profile nominations to the Supreme Court during Democrat and Republican administrations: Merrick Garland, Neil Gorsuch, Brett Kavanaugh, Amy Coney-Barrett. Garland's nomination was stalled and never moved forward. The remaining three were confirmed with relatively narrow (party line) majorities. Supreme Court nominations are win or lose in politics because Justices are seated for lifetime terms.

Large tech companies play to dominate their space and move into adjacencies of opportunity. In 1998 Amazon was a seller of books in the developing world of e-commerce, an online market that was nearly non-existent at the time. In 2022, just two decades later, Amazon is ubiquitous with leading positions in publishing, online retailing, pharmaceutical delivery, storefront operations for entrepreneurs, cloud services, and more.

Wal-Mart famously offers "everyday low prices," where shoppers often find items priced 25% less than elsewhere. Wal-Mart does this through bargaining power with their suppliers. The sheer size of Wal-Mart's operations makes them a customer too big to lose. Suppliers integrate the Wal-Mart way vertically or don't get Wal-Mart's business. Wal-Mart does not have a serious competitor of the same type. Target, Dollar Tree, and others pale in comparison. Wal-Mart competes with Amazon for customer dollars—both are playing to win. They are each winning in respective market segments; they have no close competitors.

When your customers or suppliers respond to a request for a proposal, they game it out to enhance prospects for a win. There is a cottage industry in support of improving "p-win." Companies engage in a specific price-to-win strategy that finds the sweet spot of meeting a buyer's stated requirements while maximizing opportunity and profitability. It often goes well beyond highlighting a competitive advantage and is regularly expressed internally as keeping the other competitor down.

Microsoft competed within the computer industry for decades in browser wars. Microsoft sought and established a dominant position with an inferior product. Microsoft's products were operable and installed on numerous computer brands; however, it was a monopoly. The Federal Trade Commission initially investigated Microsoft's selling practices. Twenty states and the US Department of Justice subsequently filed an antitrust suit in light of Microsoft's violations of the Sherman Anti-trust Act, which outlaws monopolies. After years of litigation, Microsoft ultimately lost its case.

In the ensuing years, more natural competitive forces eroded Microsoft's position of dominance. Microsoft was playing to win at the expense of all others and lost. They remain an industry powerhouse but suffered long-term brand damage for their business behavior.

IMPROVE THE ODDS OF A WIN

The games of chance available through lotteries have been a part of our national story since colonial times. They generate revenue while providing mild entertainment. Lotteries were in use in all 13 original colonies. Today, lotteries exist in nearly every state, and some work in concert to effectively form national lotteries such as Powerball. After winnings pay out, states typically contribute some portion of the proceeds to public works such as education or transportation.

While the games have evolved, players still exhibit the same human qualities that make the games as appealing and engaging as ever. Dreams of winning big, belief that the proceeds do good, and here's the key— *there's more than one way to win.* People buy into the lottery believing that, while they might not win big, they are likely to win *something.* While the biggest prize might have long odds, the odds of even slightly improving one's condition with a $20 scratch-off are considerably higher.[1]

Amazon Web Services (AWS) is steadily displacing Microsoft in the public sector. Microsoft had come on the scene in the 1990s with a bundled offering, Microsoft Office, and recognized that sales across entire government agencies were a lucrative enterprise sales model. Microsoft grew its federal customer base but failed to stay well connected to the customer while renewing positions for nearly 20 years. AWS cleverly approached the most classified elements of the federal public sector, the 3-letter agencies—CIA, NSA, and so forth, and surprised many industry insiders with how quickly their products and services were adopted in the federal space. Government buyers, recognizing that AWS was good enough for the most classified parts of government, readily followed suit. For much of the duration of the Trump administration, AWS and Microsoft competed for a coveted ten-billion-dollar cloud computing contract, known as the Joint Enterprise Defense Infrastructure (JEDI). The contract opportunity was ultimately canceled after numerous issues, including political influence stemming from President Trump's animus toward Amazon founder Jeff Bezos, poisoned the competition. While this is a high-profile and high-dollar value opportunity, the learning point is that AWS recognized Microsoft could be beaten; they were no longer King of the Hill.

As of this writing, the software/cloud computing/cyber environments are among the most lucrative federal opportunities. AWS outmaneuvered Microsoft to understand how federal buyers think and how they observe and often copy their peer buyer behaviors. The dominance of the federal market is not a recognizable trait of AWS.

Influencers

At a much younger age, we can recall our parents making sure the butcher didn't have a thumb on the manual scale to increase the weight of the meat, thereby creating a higher price. Smart marketers today "put their thumb on the scale" by identifying hot trends even if someone else is ahead of them.

Mercedes and BMW recognized that to grow their market share, they would need to develop models that buyers of lower-income levels could afford. At the time of the decisions, both brands were respected globally for quality and prestige. In theory, the marketing and sales effort would allow buyers who could not afford the high-end luxury model to experience the perceived luxury of the brand with a less expensive entry-level model.

Both automakers believed they were appealing to an audience that valued the brand ego appeal in these cases. That was true—until the brand became cheapened. The ubiquity of the lower-end models took value from the brand's prestige. People with the most expensive models had to wait their turn to be serviced because of all the cheaper models in line ahead of them.

In hindsight, what should have been a pronounced negative second-order effect was now evident to the automakers. Their pursuit of market dominance clouded their decisions.

Selling professional services nearly boils down to a seller of services establishing trust with a buyer and aligning the services' value with a buyer's needs. When presenting their professional services, the best sellers understand it's essential to recognize when the buyer is shifting from, "I think I want to work with Sarah," to "How can I best work with Sarah." Presenting the buyer with clearly differentiated options will allow this distinction to emerge. In Option 1, the buyer gets "good," Option 2 gets "better," and in Option 3, the buyer gets the whole enchilada. A subtle shift in the buyer's perception changes the buying dynamic. Dominance is not part of the professional services playbook.

Very few people want to pay higher prices, *but even fewer want to sacrifice value.*

WHAT MONOPOLY® CAN TEACH US

Does anyone ever win at Monopoly? It can be a fun board game (or even electronic today) around kids or a family gathering. It's also a great teaching tool of business, strategy, and winning by many gradations. Including wheeling and dealing, hugely dependent on influence. Over time, the game has been studied, and proven strategies for accumulating property and wealth by monopolizing the board have borne out. While kids playing might not fully appreciate the level of strategy and calculation the game allows, game theory experts publish proven strategies to excel at Monopoly.

Succeeding at the highest level in Monopoly requires players to continuously acquire and develop properties while maintaining sufficient cash reserves to pay various taxes and fees levied through the game. A winner ultimately emerges as other players go bankrupt and no longer have the cash to pay debts and fines. *Few master this balance of steady acquisition while preserving cash.* If the game is played long enough, monopolies will occur, and players will run out of cash. Who walks away happy? Too often, it's too few who enjoy the unsatisfying ending.

Influencers

With no small irony, the ability to manage cash even while buying properties is the same synergy needed during the Covid pandemic, when individuals and organizations which best managed and saved cash performed the best.

Creating opportunities for multiple winners could change the game's dynamic. What if there were categories of winners as opposed to only one winner? Utility owners, hoteliers, vacation property owners, or "flipping" investors are just some categories that require specific skills in real life and could be recognized separately in the game. This outcome is not the same as the "everyone gets a trophy" syndrome we see in children's sports competitions. Monopoly could acknowledge that there are multiple ways to be winners. Of course, the name of the game would need to change. Maybe Million Dollar Monopoly Influence? Just one idea!

Industries and markets have sufficient room for competition and opportunity to flourish yet behave as though only one company can win: King of the Hill. But it doesn't have to be winner take all, or best. Identifying "best" is to suggest no further improvement is possible. The cost can't be improved, and the value can't be further enhanced? It's preposterous on its face.

The sometimes-arbitrary parameters of a business competition can guide those who decide among competitive proposals that there is only one winner. It's a mistaken conclusion. It's either an element of a specific time crunch or mindless focus on the cost that overrides and clouds perspectives in business competitions. Federal buyers sometimes convince themselves to demonstrate purchasing flexibility by recognizing "best value." They apply subjectivity such as prior performance, buy-American compliance, or slavish commitment to a socio-economic set-aside to arrive at "best" in a particular set of circumstances.

CHAPTER 1 SUMMARY

Throughout Chapter 1, we present observations within your sights to which you may not be paying close enough attention. Million Dollar Influencers are attuned to their surroundings and think through the multiple factors that influence business decisions. The examples provided are simple, but only to ensure that they can be applied in situations of any level of complexity.

You are likely operating from an unaware construct that is restricting your ability to exercise influence. Regardless of your specific circumstance, whether a leader of a business, an association director, a small start-up entrepreneur, an elected official, or a senior government decision-maker, your subconscious perspectives are creeping into your decisions and responses. Are you too focused on winning because it's so ingrained in your thinking that solely winning is what's expected?

Throughout *Million Dollar Influence*, we'll show you how to observe better, and detect and understand your professional environment's conditions. With this fresh perspective, you'll soon be exercising Million Dollar Influence routinely. In Chapter 2, we'll begin by recognizing who's really in charge.

NOTE

1 It's always been an hysterical dynamic when people line up for two miles because the lottery amount is $300 million but there are no lines at all when the jackpot is ten million, as if that's inconsequential in comparison for most people's lives!

2

Accountability and authority: Two different species

WHO'S IN CHARGE? WHO'S ON FIRST?

Is it the person at the top of the organization chart? Is it the person who's been around the longest and knows where all the skeletons rest? Is it the person whose technical skills underpin the revenue? Maybe there's a rainmaker in the organization who always seems to close the big deals despite their horrible behavior. The person in charge could be any of these people, and each would likely be the wrong person, albeit for different reasons. Without clearly delineated authority there can never be accountability. *Without accountability, nobody is in charge.*

Power, be it formal or informal, can override authority, but accountability will eventually determine if stuff gets done. Understanding where authority and accountability reside in an organization chart is essential to powerful influence.

To best exercise influence, you have to interpret your environment. Any environment. No two situations are alike, but some themes run through every organizational environment. Those themes stem directly from the distribution of authority and the reconciling of accountability. When you learn to recognize the variations of authority and accountability, you can apply the most appropriate elements of influence to help move an organization to the intended destination.

DOI: 10.4324/9781003320388-2

THAT DISTANT COUSIN, RESPONSIBILITY

Responsibility is a forward-looking concept associated with ongoing oversight and control. It is often confused with blame and accountability. "Who's responsible?" or "Who did this?" or "Who let this happen?" are questions that attempt to affix blame and culpability.

Responsibility implies a degree of preparation to look after the well-being of people or an entity. The pilot of a commercial airliner meticulously follows procedural checklists. The responsibility of caring for passengers is so great that nothing is left to chance. The checklists assure consistency across situations such as weather conditions, passenger loading, pre-flight aircraft anomalies, and so forth. Firefighters undergo intense training and preparation before responding to the call and running into a burning building. In each case, they recognize their responsibilities and prepare in advance to carry them out.

In 1986, *New York Times* Magazine columnist William Safire cataloged the many applications of the question, "Who shot John?" It was a rhetorical question about where the blame rests. Safire posits that nobody cares "who shot John" because answering the question is about finger-pointing— the assignment of blame. Blame looks backward. For blame to thrive, confusion over authority and accountability precedes it. Blame focuses on who. Accountability captures performance. Who had the authority and responsibility that either met the standard or did not meet the standard? We'll discuss measures shortly, but accountability is a reconciling of "should have done" versus "did" or "did not do."

EXAMPLES THAT DISTINGUISH THE SUBTLETIES

In 1983, the USS Enterprise, the US Navy's first nuclear-powered aircraft carrier, returned from an 8-month deployment to its homeport in San Francisco. Star Trek actor George Takei flew aboard during the trip's final leg to celebrate this otherwise stellar 8-month deployment. Less than a mile from its berth, the 90,000-ton ship slipped out of the shipping channel and ran soft aground during a fog. The ship sat lodged in the muck for hours, within sight of waiting families, as nine tugs worked to get the ship free of the sand bar. "We've named a new drink-Enterprise on the rocks," said Takei to the amusement of others. In Navy parlance, this is a grounding, typically a firing offense.

The ship's Captain, R.J. Kelly, responded to press questions "offering no alibis." "I had the conn, and I am responsible," said Kelly. He acknowledged the embarrassing situation, aground within full view of the city and spectators. However, the next day's newspaper images showed hundreds of sailors assembled on the ship's flattop deck in an effort to shift thousands of pounds of weight to a more favorable position. It looked comical. Kelly would survive and subsequently promote to the rank of four-star admiral, partly due to his excellent handling of the aftermath to include his engagement with the press. The grounding did not cause serious damage to the ship and the grounding did not stem from a specific procedural failure. But this story of responsibility didn't end with this grounding incident.

Less than a decade later, Kelly was now a four-star admiral and Commander of the US Pacific Fleet, a command responsible for millions of square miles of ocean and made legendary by Admiral Chester Nimitz's holding the same position while in command during World War II. Admiral Kelly found himself at the center of the most significant cultural scandal within the Navy of modern times—he was present at the 1991 Tailhook Convention in Las Vegas, Nevada. The Tailhook Association celebrates carrier aviation, the planes of which use a tailhook to catch the arresting gear when landing on an aircraft carrier. During this convention recurring, raucous, sexually explicit, and criminal conduct by military attendees became clear. Kelly was the senior naval aviator present at the convention. While not implicated in personal wrong-doing, Kelly's role as the aviation community leader carried special responsibilities to include setting the tone. He would be forced into retirement early.

One could argue that it was a time of shifting social mores, and today the misconduct would be discovered more quickly. Times had changed; the Navy had not. The US Navy proved incapable of investigating itself, and the multi-year investigation of Tailhook became further embroiled with political overtones.

Ultimately, the Secretary of the Navy, Chief of Naval Operations, fourteen flag officers, and hundreds of naval aviators' careers ended abruptly. The impact of their failures to promote good order and discipline would plague the US Navy for a generation. Purging an organization so dependent on developing its leadership from within would cause a leadership void that took years to fill. After all, it takes time to build the experience required to replace years of experience. Both scenarios convey the concept of responsibility; the Tailhook outcomes link responsibility to accountability. Things happened that should not have, and were within the reasonable control of those with authority to do something about it.

In June 2019, during an early Democratic presidential primary debate, 37-year-old former Mayor of Indianapolis, Pete Buttigieg, stunned the political punditry with a headline-making response. He was asked by the moderator why the Indianapolis police force remained so disproportionately white despite his claims he had made it a priority. Buttigieg responded bluntly and without hesitation, "Because I couldn't get it done." Social media lit up immediately. He had violated a cardinal rule of politics by failing to control his message. The quote and focus on race in Indianapolis dogged him for the remainder of his candidacy.

At this moment, early in a national-level political career seen by many as having great potential, Buttigieg reveals his military ethos. He takes direct responsibility without mincing his words. The two-time Mayor previously served as an intelligence officer in the Naval Reserves and deployed to Afghanistan during his tenure as Mayor. He understood the question, and while not helpful to him politically, he defaulted to military training—he owned it. (Just as he had candidly talked about being gay for years.) As Mayor, he was responsible and had the authority to make changes. His admitted failure to generate a result demonstrates him taking accountability.

In October 2021, the USS Connecticut, a Seawolf-class submarine and one of only three of this type in the US inventory collided with an "unidentified seamount below the surface of the South China Sea." The security classification of submarine operations will prevent the public from ever knowing precisely what happened. However, we know that damage to the submarine was not the only casualty. Less than three weeks later, the command leadership team—the top three of the boat—were removed and replaced on the same day. The commanding officer, executive officer, and command master chief were all relieved of their duties due to their seniors' "loss of confidence."

The ensuing and swift investigation identifies "sound judgment, prudent decision-making, and adherence to required procedures in navigation planning, watch team execution and risk management could have prevented the incident." The accountability, as is the military tradition at sea, is absolute. Unfortunately, similar "losses of confidence" occur across the military services in any given year. The reasons vary but most often involve failure to adhere to procedures that result in equipment damage, injury or death, or failures in personal conduct. The key here is that accountability lives in the culture,[1] and people of all ranks bear witness to its routine enforcement. Those in authority with responsibility for oversight and control failed to meet prescribed standards and follow procedures. Subsequently, there was accountability.

BUSINESS ADAPTATIONS

In the 1950s and 1960s, International Business Machines (IBM) was a leader in the post-war era and business boom of the initial economic recovery in the United States. The transition from mainframe computers to the integration of smaller computers with common software systems foreshadowed changes to the industry. The culture at IBM was very recognizable and compared favorably to the military. Dark suits, white shirts, thin ties, and tight haircuts were a recognizable IBM uniform in business circles of the day (sounds military, doesn't it?). Organizational charts mirrored military structure with planning and strategy groups figuring prominently. Over time, the bureaucracy nearly sank the company as it struggled to adapt in the 1990s. Today, IBM is known for its expertise in consulting, which provides most of its profit, having changed its focus and culture.

IBM was and is in the information exchange business, not the business machine business, and they've recognized that. Dyson isn't in the vacuum cleaner business, it's in the air flow business. What business are you in? How are you exerting influence?

The post-war era saw other large companies follow the military order, fueled by the teachings of Peter Drucker, among others. Sears, General Motors, and General Electric built their management structures around objectives and a hierarchical organization chart. The bureaucracies that support this vision rely on positional authority; management functions implement through positional leadership. Today, none of those companies look anything like they did in 1980, 2000, or even 2010. Amazon obliterated

Sears. General Motors is belatedly moving toward electrification, but its organizational bloat and unions hinder progress. General Electric is no longer among the Dow Jones Industrial Average, is on life support, and is a mere shadow of its former self continuing to shed segments in 2021. The bureaucracies of hierarchical authorities threatened each.

In the 1970s through 1990s, matrixed organizations became the rage. Again, adopting a practice developed in the military and aerospace and defense industry, matrix management allows sharing resources across functions and products and offers an appealing approach to managing overhead by sharing costs. However, matrix management also requires that individuals report to multiple bosses through the different functions or products to which they're assigned. *Authorities are weak and accountability is weaker.*

General Stanley McChrystal, Former Commander of International and US Forces in Afghanistan, wrote the best-seller *Team of Teams* and captured the imaginations of business leaders with its tales of wartime success. Before his final leadership role in Afghanistan, McChrystal famously succeeded in bringing together a Joint Special Operations Command replete with experts from across government: FBI, Justice, CIA, etc. It was a novel approach credited with bringing all available force to bear on the most complex challenges of tracking down global terrorists. The collective effort brought Saddam Hussein to justice.

While business leaders could imagine a similar construct working in their company, the military concept of operational control doesn't translate. The US military has finely tuned procedures to transfer operational control of units. With such transfer comes a commensurate shift of both authority and accountability. When operational control transfers, orders flow from the new boss and are executed as officially required. This critical ingredient is often missing in the business environment's adaptation of this military concept of forming their own Teams of Teams.

Today's edgiest software companies adopt agile management practices first introduced in 2000. Agile is a mindset that promotes continuous improvement through the incremental development of software. Its principal feature mitigates risk by assuring a project doesn't get too far along in development only to learn of a crucial glitch introduced into the software months ago. Agile is well established in commercial enterprises and industry. In government, it's a foreign concept. The bureaucracy of government is anathema to agile's most basic premise—rapid adaptation.

Scrum thrives within an agile environment. Scrum is a derivative of matrix thinking, but its design captures employee energy and assigns responsibilities. Scrum management draws on the rugby concept of a scrum where teams are consciously interlocked with each teammate's upper bodies, arms, and heads, working together to gain leverage and position. The coordination of the collective effort allows the team to progress. Scrum differs from matrix management with its defined roles that capture the essence of authority. A Scrum product owner is the liaison between the team and the customer. A Scrum master keeps the team on task. Scrum team members are equals and implement tasks consistent with their abilities.

Other leadership and management trends and fads have come and gone. Servant leadership, transformational leadership, transactional management, pseudo-transformational leadership, situational and behavioral approach, managerial grid theory, the one-minute manager, and more are just some of the many. None have genuinely withstood time, and organizational management remains an evolving concept. But the ingredients of authority and accountability remain required elements of any organization and management construct.

Many small and mid-sized companies cling to order despite their desperate desire to be new and edgy. Look through most corporate directories, and you will find the tell-tale sign that also remains a relic of the military hierarchy—the chief of staff. This catch-all role can vary among applications but often performs for a principal as a deputy, alter-ego, executive assistant, *consigliere*, enforcer, or some amalgamation thereof. Chiefs of staff are also familiar in government agencies and congressional offices and perform a role tailored to the peculiarities of the principal. In short, their authority depends, and their accountabilities are unique to the relationship with the principal. This position is a crutch that should be universally banned.

AUTHORITY DOESN'T HAVE TO MEAN BUREAUCRACY

We like titles. Titles can provide a sense of structure in a company. Vice president, senior vice president, executive vice president, director, senior director, or managing director, manager, assistant manager, or associate.

They bring a feel-good sense of order. Unsatisfied with service in a department store, we may ask, "I'd like to see the manager." Banks are well known to liberally dispense the title of vice president to give customers the sense they are dealing with an authority figure.

We complicate the order that titles might imbue within a company by further categorizing teams, committees, departments, sectors, segments, and functional areas. Again, we think we're reinforcing order, but in fact, we create bureaucracy. Sometimes those with the title and the authority to make decisions dilute their effect even further with the ultimate creature of decision-making within a bureaucracy—the committee. Informal power, the granting of authority through one's natural leadership or charisma, can complicate any organization, but nowhere does it manifest more obviously than within a committee.

Note that "committees" are not teams, and most organizations, from Congress to a car dealership chain, actually have committees. "Team building" usually fails because you can't "team build" a committee.

When authority properly accompanies a role, it bestows decision-making capacities associated with the position. Authority can pass from one level to another or various team members. Think of it in the same way a sheriff might deputize a "deputy." The authority allows for the carrying out of order and enforcing the law. In business settings, authority can be complicated by aspects of the organization or by power and control exerted by an individual.

Accountability, on the other hand, is not something readily delegated. President Harry Truman is often associated with the phrase, "The buck stops here," as it was emblazoned on a desk plaque for him by a friend. The phrase captured there was no one above him to which "the buck" could pass. He was responsible (looking forward) and accountable (the backward and objective look at the result).

HOW IS ACCOUNTABILITY LEARNED?

Bobby Bowden was among the winningest college football coaches of all time. During his decades in coaching, he rose to national prominence while coaching at Florida State University. His personal and public image was an irascible country coach long on street smarts and grounded in his faith and family. The image of a humble family man and preacher stood in contrast to some infamous off-field conduct by his players. Throughout his coaching tenure, numerous players made headlines from simple curfew infractions to criminal conduct that would gain the attention of the US Attorney. None were severe impediments to his teams' winning.

During Bowden's winning streak height while preparing for the 2002 Sugar Bowl against Virginia Tech in New Orleans, Sebastian Janikowski, a walk-on kicking phenom whose family had emigrated from Poland, violated curfew with some teammates. The press was relentless questioning Bowden, "Will he play? Will he start? Can you win without him?" Bowden quipped, "I have an international rule. Now, if I had a player commit murder, well then I would have to let him go." He re-anchored the discussion to persuade the media they had lost perspective. Bowden's coaching peers saw it as the continuation of a string of examples of Bowden's willingness to look the other way with off-field player infractions in the interest of winning games. Bowden's nemesis at the arch-rival University of Florida, Steve Spurrier, would coin the phrase Free Shoes University, referencing the theft of athletic shoes by some star players at the local mall that appeared to go unpunished. Lack of accountability hurt the program.

Business scandals emerge with enough regularity to confirm behavioral patterns of executives and reveal the extraordinary pressures of the roles. The financial collapse of 2008 was completely recognizable in hindsight, yet unfolded in plain view. Increasingly risky sub-prime loans were granted to creditors without the means to pay for homes appraised far above their true value. Loans were subsequently bundled, repackaged, and sold above their value. The house of cards ultimately collapsed causing a global financial crisis, not to mention a severe crisis of confidence in the financial institutions themselves. A now seemingly quaint, but for its time massive, government infusion of $700 billion into the financial system would stem the economy from collapse.

Entire segments within the financial industry saw the faults within the system, in some cases as early as 2004–2005. Yet the division of authorities among market makers, financial institutions, government regulators, and myriad service providers attached to the financial apparatus hindered any one entity from taking responsibility in advance. Lehman Brothers was among the more notable institutions to go under and confirms how instantiated the diffusion of responsibility had become.

Bernie Madoff, who defrauded investors of billions of dollars with his Ponzi scheme, went unchecked for years, despite the detailed whistle-blower actions of Harry Markopolos as many as six years prior to Madoff's arrest in 2005. Madoff would consistently report uncommonly high returns for his clients over the course of decades, something clearly extraordinary. Looking back, government regulators at the time of the unraveling claim limited resources available to keep up with the fast-moving world of private investment. In this case, influence is at play on all sides, for good and evil. Madoff's understanding of what regulators needed to see, and regulators' discomfort with rocking the boat of a high-profile investor serving even higher-profile celebrity clients. The Dodd-Frank Wall Street Reform and Consumer Protection Act became law in 2010—a reactive step intended to restate where responsibilities, authorities, and accountabilities reside in the financial system.

Leonardo DiCaprio's over-the-top portrayal of disgraced stockbroker Jordan Belfort in *The Wolf of Wall Street* was nominated for multiple academy awards and earned DiCaprio the best actor award at the Golden Globe Awards. The movie's theme is winning at all costs and that people are stooges who would buy into his mirage of success. Jordan Belfort was ultimately brought to justice and jailed, having broken the law and violated myriad ethical standards.

Jeffrey Epstein alluded justice for years for his criminal sexual acts with minors. For nearly 15 years, from 2004 to 2019, Epstein was charged with felonies, released, jailed briefly, then released again through extraordinary deals. For a portion of that time, Epstein was identified as a Level III sex offender, meaning he was a high risk for a repeat offense, yet he mostly remained out of prison. During a relatively brief imprisonment in 2008–2009, Epstein was granted a work-release six days per week for up to 12 hours per day. During another period of probation, he was allowed to travel by private jet to the Caribbean. The Miami Herald identifies one extraordinary episode of special treatment granted by US Attorney Alexander Acosta as a "deal of a lifetime" in which Epstein received immunity. The Palm Beach Sheriff's Office under whose local jurisdiction most crimes took place, proved powerless to overcome myriad grants, exceptions, and contortions of the justice system that took place at the federal level.

Epstein died in jail in New York City under highly suspicious circumstances in 2019. Several high-profile lawyers defended Epstein along the way in exchange for handsome retainers and notoriety. The aforementioned US Attorney Acosta was forced to resign from his position as US Secretary of Labor in 2019 when the political heat associated with the immunity deal he previously brokered became too hot for even President Trump to retain him. Over one dozen young women testify to the clear criminal conduct by Epstein, yet his actions went unchecked and he mostly walked among us as he exerted unknown influence throughout the legal system.

This sort of breakdown of responsibility, accountability, and authority is extreme. However, when one looks at it through the lens of influence it's clear to see influence at play. For reasons that may never be clear in this case, some circumstances caused people with responsibility and authority to deflect both responsibility and accountability. What shifted the case from the hands of the Palm Beach Sherriff's Office to the US Attorney? What explains so many exceptions to be made in the treatment of someone charged multiple times with felony sexual misconduct? What motivates a US Attorney General to extend a "deal of a lifetime?" We can't know that precisely. What we do know is that at every level of the multiple cases against Epstein, people made decisions for good or bad. Recognizing influence in its most raw form represents a learning point. Influence is ultimately about interactions with people.

Hurricanes are seasonal events for which contingencies exist. In late August 2005, Hurricane Katrina skipped across Florida as a Tropical Storm, then quickly intensified as it rolled north through the Gulf of Mexico. Katrina came ashore as a Category 5 hurricane, affecting several southern states. New Orleans took the brunt as levees failed and flooding took weeks to control. Power outages, human suffering, and rescue efforts were captured on television for a nation to watch in disbelief. Nearly 2,000 people died, not due to the initial storm strike, but from the failures to integrate a state and federal response. President George Bush famously missed the mark in grasping his responsibility and accountability. He had nearly completely delegated the federal response to the Federal Emergency Management Agency (FEMA) and failed to coordinate clearly with then-Governor of Louisiana, Kathleen Babineaux Blanco. His now infamous quote to then-FEMA Administrator Michael Brown, "Brownie, you're doing a heck of a job," doomed the moment for Bush. President Bush had delegated authority but was still responsible and ultimately accountable for the failures.

Other governors learned from the Katrina moment. Florida Governor Jeb Bush earned praise for his multiple well-coordinated hurricane responses during his terms of office. He recognized both coordinating the efforts and making sure people knew he was coordinating efforts, was necessary. They were responsibilities of the office, for which he had the authority to take contingent actions.

In 2012, "Superstorm" Sandy came ashore in New Jersey at Category 2 with relatively low wind strength. However, the storm measured over 1,000 miles in diameter, meaning historic rain and flooding would accompany the aptly identified Superstorm. Governor Chris Christie recognized the need for federal support and welcomed his political adversary President Barack Obama to New Jersey to demonstrate mutual support. Both pols knew they needed to work together to save lives and orchestrate a fulsome response. Each took short-term heat for working together. They were chastised for being seen in a sideways embrace that the press reported as a hug. In reality, it was a handshake with their opposite hands on the other man's shoulder; much more of a "thanks for being here" moment. Each understood his responsibilities.

How are the lessons of authority and accountability learned? In the scenarios above, the learning occurs within the organizational culture: a military service, an industry, a sports league and team, a community, or a political environment. The basics are taught in some schools, but not all schools. Transference of this knowledge most often occurs within organizations and through observation and the school of hard knocks. Too often the learning takes a negative form, learning through the failure of others: failed companies, lost jobs, lives injured or destroyed, and legal prosecution of criminal conduct.

MIGHTY MEASURES

What are standards and goals? Think of a continuum that connects the two. A standard is a minimum, below which we don't want to fall. A goal is aspirational; a target we may reach, but we may not. It's great to achieve a goal and can be cause for legitimate celebration. We can raise the bar higher and aspire to an even loftier next goal when we reach a goal. Standards can be raised but not lowered without express cause.

The postal service keeps lowering delivery standards and the public continually distrusts it.

Authority is not so much measured as its existence is understood. It is inherent in a role or position. The contracts officer has the authority to obligate funds up to a specified amount for authorized purchase orders. The sales rep has the authority to agree to a rough-order-of-magnitude price schedule to frame an initial deal. However, a definitive contract where price specifications are more tightly defined may be outside the authority of the sales rep. Such bounds of authority are knowable and codified in words and actions.

The measure of accountability is more typically assigned a pass or fail grade. Standards are met or not met. The measure of accountability requires a look back over how well we did or didn't do. Did the sales team meet the quota? If not, there is a way to account for how or why the team did not meet the quota. The how or why when connected to the who or whom, measure accountability.

CHAPTER 2 SUMMARY

Those capable of exercising Million Dollar Influence know how to interpret their environment in a way that identifies both the distribution of authority and the ownership inherent in accountability. Salespeople and consultants learn to identify the actual economic buyer quickly. They have to get good at this, or they lose and waste time. That's time that could support efforts with other buyers. With an outsider's perspective, great consultants can readily identify where a disconnect between authority and accountability exists. The remaining time in a consulting engagement then focuses on teaching the team how to align these concepts to the business objectives. When working with organizations to shape outcomes or new positions, applying Million Dollar Influence means recognizing who has formal or informal power to enable decisions of the actual decider. The concepts apply to business enterprises, political offices, and business associations, alike.

Leaders in business and politics become experts at recognizing the distinctions of responsibility, authority, and accountability through experience. Some survive the learning environment in the tests of life, while others fall victim and stop ascending in organizations. Identifying these characteristics is learnable and can be honed with practice. Million Dollar Influence recognizes how the framework can be adapted in any scenario. The most successful leaders understand this early in their careers and strive to teach it to others.

Emotional IQ, or EQ, is associated with an ability to "read the room." A Million Dollar Influencer has high EQ because they can decipher concepts such as, who's in charge, who should be in charge, or why are we doing something or not doing something? Authority and accountability are at the center of understanding these questions. When applied in a specific organization, one can evaluate where leverage will improve a condition. In Chapter 3, we'll explore the application of leverage and why Archimedes believed that, with a lever, he could rule the world.

That lever is the identification and mastery of influence.

NOTE

1 Let's define "culture" here as "that set of beliefs which governs behavior."

3

Arm wrestling is about leverage

When you watch two highly skilled arm wrestlers move into their initial setup, you recognize there's much more to the match than the strength of their arms. Pure muscle strength is a factor, but it often is not the *deciding factor*. Technique influences the win as often as brute strength.

Before the match begins, each arm wrestler seeks a specific starting position, squared off to their opponent with at least one foot on the floor. Confirming an initial grip position establishes the mutual engagement and that a starting point is now imminent. Keeping one's opposite hand on the peg is not only a cardinal rule of the sport; it allows a critical point of leverage. Influencing business outcomes is about gaining purchase or leverage within a set of legal and ethical constraints. Million Dollar Influence recognizes the advantages of leverage.

YOU USE YOUR ENTIRE BODY AND ALL YOUR WEAPONRY

Archimedes was a Greek mathematician and scientist who lived over 2,000 years ago. The understanding of experimental science with pulleys, screws, winches, and most famously, the lever and fulcrum, expanded through his discoveries. Applying geometric principles, Archimedes confirmed the amplifying impact of a lever applied to a fulcrum.

We might recognize a fulcrum from the teeter-totter on the playground. A lever and fulcrum can help move something sizeable with considerably less effort than a deadlift. Levers exist all around us, and we hardly notice scissors, wheelbarrows, crowbars, and hammer claws, for example. It's easy to overlook the simplicity of the lever's function.

DOI: 10.4324/9781003320388-3

Influencers

Give me a lever and I can move the world.

—Archimedes

The arm wrestlers above cannot use additional tools to gain leverage. Arm wrestling is a come-as-you-are sport. What's lost on some observers is the smarts that accompany the brawn. You may need to change your level of preparation and situational awareness for your actual influence to emerge.

The military teaches and hones the concept of situational awareness (SA). Learning to notice one's surroundings and recognize changes to the environment can mean the difference in mission success or failure. It applies across all services and is most prominent at the tactical level of operations. Losing SA, failing to recognize something significant is changing or not as it should be, is usually the root cause when things go wrong in the field. Learning to identify levers and the associated fulcrum requires developing a better sense of SA.

Pilots are quite good at managing SA through a combination of repetitive training, a culture that demands excellence, and recognizing the window of focus during critical periods of a mission. Scanning instruments, kneeboards of details, the external environment, and multiple radio channels simultaneously require the ability to recognize subtle differences readily and act on them instinctively. *You do this in your car when someone slams on their brakes in front of you.*

Organizations have risen or fallen due to their SA. Sears didn't realize the buyers' preferences had changed. Dyson realized they were actually in the air movement business.

The best athletes in team sports can quickly scan the playing field or court and recognize how what's unfolding fits or doesn't fit the pattern of the play—or the opportunity that presents when a play breaks down. Fractions of seconds make the difference in basketball and hockey. Working together, players quickly set and shift plays that either advance their position offensively or break their opponent's movement or tempo defensively.

NFL quarterbacks succeed by their speed of decision-making, where a split second can mean seeing an opening before it has fully formed, allowing the ball to meet the player at the precise moment of arrival. The great coach, Vince Lombardi, urged his players to "run to daylight," meaning opposing players had left that space.

Some great college-level players don't display the same processing speed and therefore can't transition to the professionals. Various levers help force the plays to unfold in sequence. Variations of picks, feints, reverses, and distractions allow the placement of a fulcrum on which the play gains leverage. Athletes hone these skills through practice. They continually work on their craft with the support of competent coaches. "Reps and sets" build muscle memory, allowing subconscious competence to thrive.

An appropriately positioned lever will consistently outperform the hammer and vise-grips you may be using in your business engagements. Great organizations don't hammer the competition into submission, they use leverage to outmaneuver them.

Blunt instruments dull the senses and don't allow for fine craftsmanship. Just as Archimedes could examine surroundings to form logical conclusions, so can you! Million Dollar Influence recognizes that it's more than a personable nature and a firm handshake that advances business objectives. Your business environment counterparts yield clues throughout the entirety of an engagement.

Some examples of levers you may not be considering include the following:

- Qualification of supplier networks. Buyers (and especially the government) are precise about where components originate, and assembly takes place.
- Speed of delivery, performance, turnaround, time to market
- Workforce training—yours and theirs
- Prior performance
- Revolutionary methodology
- Geographic location
- Order quantities
- Ability to fund a large order
- Market position
- Economic forecast
- Shareholder concerns
- Boards of Directors
- New hire(s)
- Political environment such as changes in administration

- Process knowledge
- Access to government funding
- Changes in policy
- Ambiguity in the stated requirement
- The need for a near-term win
- Patience or impatience
- Scientific discovery
- Expiration of a patent
- Guarantee of a specific period of exclusivity
- Use of third-party advocacy
- Recognizing decision influencers and decision enablers

Influencers

Here's just one example from the list: third-party advocacy. The world of sales today is one of evangelism, where other people promote you. Your lever is the ability to bring your evangelists together with your prospects.

This list is the tip of the iceberg and relates to your ability to examine and identify potential points of leverage. Your business counterpart reveals this information directly and indirectly on an ongoing basis. Are you noticing, or could you be their fulcrum, adding to their leverage?

THE OTHER PERSON HAD YOUR GOOD IDEA

There are no new ideas. There are technological advancements, of course, and scientific discovery does yield new thinking. However, in a world of nearly six billion people, do you think your idea, or that of your five- or even 100-person team is so unique that others could not imagine it? Get over yourself. You and your team may be great, but don't confuse that with being unique.

You may have something relatively new. It may have a patent or be far along in the patenting process. Perhaps you've even registered a trademark to stake out your competitive territory. Those regulatory tools have a place but won't preserve your position of advantage for long. A competitor might well have been simultaneously developing the same concept on a slightly different timeline.

If your new thing is that great, you can be sure the "fast follower" copycat is right behind you. Samsung has built an empire on the concept, with 2021 revenue exceeding 60 billion dollars. Accept that you'll need to adapt and innovate continuously and, good as you are, your product or idea is not safely unique.

You and your team spend days preparing for a sales opportunity with a qualified buyer whom you know you can serve well. You craft your message, rehearse every transition in your presentation, and memorize your lines right down to the scripted humor. You walk into a buyer's waiting area not knowing you are following on the heels of a competitor's presentation. You see through the glass walls the remnants of the prior meeting. Charts, and maybe a small prototype on the table, look much like yours. How did they get our idea? Observing the smiles and handshakes confirm that the competitor thinks they were able to deliver and have this opportunity sewn up. As you set up to present, you notice you are starting to sweat a bit. Your small talk is weak; your throat is a bit tighter. Your nervousness starts to reveal, and your confidence wanes.

As you begin your presentation, you can feel the stiffness in your delivery, and the choreographed transitions fall flat. Your teammates begin to look at the buyer, then at the table, then at their shoes. Eye contact with the audience fails you. You feel yourself shrinking, and your presentation sinks.

The military instills a concept at the very core of its planning processes. *"No plan survives contact with the enemy."*[1] This concept lives in every community of every military service. No matter how hard we train, plan, or script various scenarios, the circumstances will always contain some variable for which there was no plan. The unexpected can do one of two things: (1) derail your plan as in the presentation above, or (2) present an opportunity to apply some form of leverage.

The value of sets and reps in sports and military training frees up brainpower to think at the moment. The presenter above was exercising conscious competence to think through a scripted event. Under the pressure of the moment, for which their preparation is inadequate, they clung to the script as if it were their life ring. It was an anvil. The real culprit in this scenario is the closed-mindedness of not being prepared for the unexpected.

Had the team gone in with a range of possibilities instead of a singular point solution, they could pivot at the moment. Drawing attention to the elephant in the room, the prototype on the table could have opened the conversation differently. What if the presenter opened with, "I couldn't help but notice ACME's widget on the table. What did you think?" If you knew anything of ACME's widget, you'd be able to comment on the merits or challenges with their approach. At a minimum, you would learn something new from the buyer. Relying on your uniqueness closes off creativity. Million Dollar Influencers know when to depart from the script. Let's look further at how additional subtleties can move you toward a win.

Case Study: The communications strategy

I was at the offices of a major insurance company which had acquired another of the same size. Five consultants had been brought in to make presentations to the executive vice president and his staff for a communications strategy, and how to inform employees of progress. All five were known by repute to the vice president. Because my name starts with "W" I was last in the alpha order.

I had watched four groups walk into the conference room with easels, projectors, and handouts. Each had a minimum of four people. Finally, about 90 minutes later, my time came at 5 p.m.

The room had the smell of exhaustion. I walked in alone, with only my Filofax planner, nothing else. The executive asked me wearily what I would propose as a communications strategy moving forward.

I said, "Don't tell anyone anything," and shut up. The room was as still as a tomb. The vice president finally said, "What are you talking about?"

"Do you know which offices will close?" I asked.

"No, that's in the hands of the board."

"Do you know which executives will be retained and which released?"

"No, that's very sensitive, and we have a committee working on it."

"Do you know which compensation plan you'll use?"

"No, but we have a compensation consulting firm studying it."

"So," I pointed out, "you don't know anything, so don't tell them anything. Simply be open to questions and tell employees you'll answer them as soon as you have the answers. Encourage questions, don't provide empty information."

"That's counterintuitive," he said.

"Yes, it is."

Ten minutes later we shook hands on what would be a $250,000 communications "strategy." This is SA at work.

WIN IN A CLOSE MATCH, DON'T BREAK FINGERS

A close match in business can look like a very tight set of requirements, including time, cost, and material constraints. There are myriad things within your control when faced with what looks like a very competitive scenario. Your finesse of the situation will stem from your prior planning and will prevent poor performance. Finesse allows you to take bold positions that you convey with thoughtful words and without waving blunt tools. To apply finesse, you need to be an expert at recognizing your and your counterpart's *points of differentiation*.

Understanding your points of differentiation and applying them to a range of solutions and outcomes can help your business counterpart see the relationship from a new perspective. But you have to identify them. You can't expect that your audience is engaged thoroughly enough to identify these for themselves. Even if the product you sell is as commoditized as a paperclip, you must draw out points of differentiation to highlight the competitive advantage. Size, color, coating, tensile strength, the curvature of the end, order quantity, delivery date, price escalators, package bundles, and logo applications are just the start. These descriptions can be made without badmouthing a competitor by name and allow you to demonstrate both knowledge and grace.

When the National Security Team briefs the President of the United States, there is always a range of options on the table. "Mr. President, you can implement any of these options to achieve an appropriate outcome; each has merit and second-order effects. They are as follows." After explaining at least three options and their implications, you recommend or ask what they think. Allowing other people, even the President of the United States, to proffer their thoughts provides space in the discussion. This process doesn't have to take long, but it's critical to let the decider feel like they are deciding.

Influencers

Most people think "victory" or "success" is a single option, a bullseye. In reality, a range of options can all provide success. This is a rheostat, not an on/off switch. The search for a "perfect" solution undermines the ability to achieve excellent solutions.

This manner of high-level discussion allows for additional discovery in both directions and doesn't force an end with a single-point decision. The range of options allows decision-makers to perceive that they control the decision. Getting comfortable with a degree of ambiguity in the back-and-forth takes a little practice. However, when mastered, it will allow some maneuvering room while the conversation still advances to your preferred objective. The effect is subtle and doesn't feel like you've painted the decider into a corner. In this case, you are leveraging the decision-maker's ego. You've painted them into a room, not a corner!

Courtesies in business are nearly a lost art. The hand-written thank you note will always convey respect, for example, even when delivered by the US Postal Service! But long before the time for the note, courtesy shows through preparation and alignment of expectations.

Going into a meeting where the expectations are not aligned wastes everyone's time. Confirming the intent of a business meeting will save time and failure work[2]. Is the meeting for a general introduction, consideration of alternatives, hammering out contractual language, or making a final decision? Each will require different levels of preparation and perhaps different participants.

In school, we may learn that the average adult attention span is 30–45 minutes. We also learn as young executives to have an "elevator pitch" at the ready, a way to quickly blurt out who you are and what you do. Both are wrong. The magic number is eight minutes.

Gene uses his eight-minute rule of messaging (SM) across all meetings with industry, the executive branch, and Congress. It's a sure-fire way to balance the complexity of a message with the reality of schedule constraints and focus. If a meeting typically books for 30 minutes, you can't use all 30. Worse, you can't go over the time allocated. An eight-minute message has four parts: they are identification of the issue, a brief background on how we got here, a short discussion of options, and a recommendation. When those four elements are conveyed promptly, you will be a hero, because you showed respect for the other person's time. Best of all, you bring forth clarity. *Here you use the clock as leverage.*

Are there other influencers available to deploy or incorporate into your plan? Decision mapping applies to understanding organization charts of businesses, terrorist groups, or the mafia. Knowing who the decision-makers take counsel from can be helpful. In government, the actual decision-maker is rarely one person.

Decisions by committee or a series of committees are the norm. In presidential decisions such as above, there is an entire "national security decision-making apparatus" in place. Your business counterpart may not have such an elaborate mechanism, but the person you think is likely "the decider" is subject to powerful influencers in their orbit. Those influencers or enablers of deciders can be within industry trade associations, compliance requirements, policy constraints, or family members in a family-owned company. The variables are endless, but does your perspective of your business counterpart even allow for these variables? You can leverage any variable in the decision process.

Your preparation and consideration are essential differentiators that will influence outcomes. Can you see that while it looks like strength carries the day in the arm-wrestling match, the arm wrestler goes into the match with a much more complete understanding of the format? Incorporating solution ranges, an outline of how you'll spend your targeted eight minutes, consideration of additional influences, and a mindset of openness collectively add to your influence.

ADVANTAGE SERVER

How many meetings have you sat through and watched as one person sat back and took it all in before revealing their position on the matter at hand? Some leaders subscribe to letting others speak first, not hindering the candid flow of ideas around a table. What we're describing is different—an ambush mentality. Peers at the table lay in wait to either knock down others' ideas or outshine others in front of the boss. It's a petty tactic.

Suppose you sell to the federal or state governments. Have you attended an industry day where the acquisition professionals of the government team tried to describe what they wanted but couldn't articulate in the request for information (RFI) sent to the industry? Government buyers often gather industry representatives in a structured effort to force a dialogue that promotes equal access to the government buyer. In those open sessions, some companies lurk on the margins and stalk their competition with no intention of revealing anything to others, let alone the government buyer. So concerned about losing a perceived, or even minuscule, competitive advantage that they share nothing in an open industry group setting.

In professional teaching sessions, Alan routinely sees people hold themselves back from an opportunity to learn in front of others "in the moment" and unscripted. It's rare for someone new to Alan's established teaching community to put themselves on the hot seat for a role-play or impromptu interview at the first opportunity. It takes people a while to recognize that learning by doing at the moment and in a safe environment is far more beneficial than learning from hard knocks in the buyer's office.

The scenarios above describe an underlying fear and weakness that is unmistakable. For the individuals above, the fear of being seen as not having the "right" or even an acceptable answer is so strong it inhibits their ability to participate most effectively. Above, the fear compounds with an insidious pursuit of the win at the expense of others.

Influencers

No one knows how long a lobster can live or how big it can get. They've caught lobsters at 80 pounds and a few thought to be 100 years old. Lobsters have an exoskeleton (shell) so they must molt to grow (shed the shell). They are vulnerable while they do this. But they grow a new larger shell and become stronger. You must be vulnerable at times in order to grow. This is Alan's "Lobster Principle."

These weak players fail to recognize the advantage inherent in going first, without the influence of others. In business communications being the first to present can do several things: (1) establish your immutable expertise, (2) pleasantly surprise your counterpart, and (3) decisively shape the next moves of the conversation. Control of the tempo of the meeting with your choice of language and pace is an advantage you can leverage unless you fail to take it. (And in Alan's case study of the insurance company earlier, you see that going last can be successful if you're also the first to provide a unique point of view.)

In tennis, the server has a distinct advantage to control the critical first move of the game (as in chess, when you play the white pieces, as well). Competence and confidence are required to do this well. Going first has no advantage if you're not capable of rising to the moment. If you don't take that risk, this book won't help you either. Million Dollar Influence is learnable and can improve with practice.

CHAPTER 3 SUMMARY

The competition and adrenaline of business can be invigorating. The most successful people in sales thrive on the energy of engagement. This chapter opens the door to multiple differentiators and subtleties that are a part of the competitive landscape but too often aren't used to full advantage.

Million Dollar Influencers seek leverage, allowing the factors at hand to do the heavy lifting for you. Knowing the value of planning and appropriate use of an outline instead of a script will reveal countless points of leverage you may be missing. In Chapter 4 we'll help you recognize the cardinal rule of improvisational comedy—accepting what's given!

NOTES

1 The sports analogy is Mike Tyson's famous observation that everyone has a winning plan entering the ring until they are hit in the jaw.
2 Failure work is work that needs to be done because originally it wasn't done well enough. Creating failure work for yourself is terrible. Performing failure work that someone else created is horrid.

4

The improv game

Business developers and sales teams like to use colored hats to name the teams who will "game out" business scenarios: red, black, and white hat teams exist in many large companies. Millions of days per year are lost as teams attempt to work through contingencies of a presentation. PowerPoint slides are edited and rehearsed *ad nauseum*, carefully synchronizing slide animations with a finely rehearsed script.

The problem with this rote memorization of the customer encounter is the utter failing to be present "in the moment." Forcing a scripted sequence without allowing for the necessary flow of a real conversation will stifle progress. Rule number one of improv is to accept what your partner gives you. The same applies in a business conversation.

If an improv partner says, "How did we get in this cab," the other person doesn't say, "We're not in a cab." The reply would be something like "Shut up and take the next left."

ALWAYS STAY IN THE MOMENT

Improvisation dates back to ancient Rome when actors would take the stage without a script and rehearsal. As a form of comedy, its perfection over time also sustains its popularity in generating great comedy content.

During the 1950s and 1960s, structural rules would make the form teachable. Second City Television famously formalized the improvisational process and would become a reliable pipeline of some of our best-known comedy actors at the turn of the 21st century. Nobody is suggesting

DOI: 10.4324/9781003320388-4

you need to be funnier or incorporate physical comedy into your business conversation, *but it's worth examining some of what makes improv work.*

In the early 2000s, business schools would begin to recognize the value of the skillset that makes improvisation generate unexpected outcomes while simultaneously fueling a person's confidence in ambiguous situations. Comedians Stephen Colbert and Tina Fey, when presenting more serious reflective sides of themselves, both convey that the critical transference between comedy and the workplace is getting to "yes." Allowing more space for "yes" can increase the likelihood of you getting to your desired outcome.

Salespeople who sell in situations where the buying decision is short—such as cars, furniture, mattresses, or clothes—are taught to get the prospect to say "yes" three times. You soften the exchange and build rapport to get them to say this three times.

Think about the last car you bought. While walking the lot, did you answer several questions? Easy questions anyone could answer without feeling like the seller is too intrusive. "Do you carpool kids to their activities?" "Will this be your daily driver?" "Do you use your phone for navigation?" These are soft-touch questions.

They're also psychologically sound. Robert Cialdini, in his book *Influence*, cites "consistency" as a key to influence.[1]

Think about your last trip to buy a dress. The sales clerk suggests, "That cut looks great on you. Do you like blue or would you like to try it in red? I also have it in green. Shall we see the difference?" Nothing pushy, but a presumptive dialogue that delivers a compliment while allowing you to retain the power of the decision. In neither case is the seller using a script, but they don't know for sure what your answers will be. However, they are moving the prospect toward a purchase.

Case Study: Rapid consistency

In the 1980s, I had a Mercedes 450 SLC. One day, I received a call at home from a woman:

Her: Is this Alan Weiss?
Me: Yes (no harm in admitting that).
Her: Do you own a Mercedes 450 SLC?
Me: Yes (it might be a recall).

Her: How would you like to own one of the very first car phones in
New England?
Me: (After thinking for three seconds) How quickly can you get here?

I had a car phone in every car ever since until cell phones took away the
need. Three questions to a sale using consistency.

ACCEPT WHAT YOU'RE GIVEN

Your business environment is far more complex than the scenarios above.
But the complex is not the same as complicated. Complex means you have
to break it down. The same *improvisational tools are adaptable to any business situation*. Getting to yes requires you to take what's given and not resist.

The word "no" in business should only apply to situations where legal
compliance and ethical behavior are at stake. Everything else should be a
variation on yes and acceptance. Law and policy are both means of man-
dating compliance; you can apply influence to both.

Influencers

There's always another way.
      —Kevin Costner as John Dutton in the streaming hit *Yellowstone*

"Don't fight the trainer" is a maxim in military training. Simulations take
the place of elements of a scenario that don't lend to replication. By definition, a simulation is not real. But working through the decision processes
that simulations prompt allows warfighters to effect "sets and reps" without the deadly consequences.

A hybrid of "live-virtual constructed training" is a multi-billion-dollar
industry. Tom Cruise introduced us to "Top Gun," an early version of this
hybrid methodology. Because there are elements of the training that can
appear unrealistic, it's tempting to "fight the trainer" and undervalue specific inputs. In its worst form fighting the trainer means you blame some
aspect of your flawed execution on the trainer instead of owning it for

what it was. It's the same as not accepting your improv partner's input. *It's also the same as not accepting that your business counterpart has introduced a particular constraint.*

When engaging someone from another company or within an agency, you must accept that you don't know that environment the same way as the people you are meeting. You might think you do. You might have even worked there before. But circumstances and cultures are not fixed—they shift. Think about flying a plane or driving a boat. The air and water always have some influence on them. You subtly apply stick and rudder to navigate changing currents. *You are moving in three dimensions, not two.*

Have you been misidentifying any of the business currents below that your business counterpart is steering toward you?

- Rationale that supports a particular specification
- Buying horizon (you can always accelerate it)
- Availability of a decision-maker
- Their level of understanding of your technology or capability
- Longstanding relationship with an incumbent
- Creative contract terms
- Order quantity
- Requests for pricing discounts
- Exclusivity demands
- Time constraints in any form
- Weather allowances
- Market instability
- "Supply chain" concerns—a vague reference if there ever was one
- The end-user doesn't see the need for the technology
- There is no documented requirement for a capability

The list contains improv lines waiting to be transformed by a skilled counterpart. Some could appear in what looks like a no, but you should be transforming into a yes. The variations to this list are endless and only limited by the combination of circumstances and your creativity.

One of Alan's favorite lines:

Buyer: You aren't familiar with our industry and you don't have many employees.
Alan: That's exactly why you need me!!

Case Study: Steering through uncertainty

Don Estridge of IBM was the earliest leader of IBM's entry into the personal computer market. So valued was his creativity and business sales acumen that Steve Jobs pursued him vigorously to work at Apple. Estridge was famous for acknowledging the energy one could draw when in the presence of a live customer. The full potential of the personal computer in the 1980s was unknown, yet he was guiding with broad strokes.

Estridge's gift for recognizing the importance of the people in business is legendary. Translation—the battle is half-won when you're on stage with your improv partner, and it's just a matter of working toward the yes. Jobs' recognition of another great mind *within his competitor's camp* and attempting to break barriers is also informative.

Don Estridge declined Jobs' generous offer to come to Apple because he viewed jumping ship to the competitor as disloyal. While IBM failed to displace Apple, the culture of looking for the win during a time of ambiguity is evidence of the new direction. IBM would ultimately recognize that IBM must change to adapt to the new environment. As described in Chapter 2, IBM left the hardware business and today focuses on services in the ensuing decades.

QUESTIONS TRUMP ANSWERS

Excellent questions produce more meaningful answers. To ask the most responsive questions requires an ability to absorb surroundings and encourage your counterpart to connect specifics to the more general and vice versa. "Shall we jump from this perfectly good airplane?" paints an immediate image for an improv partner and the audience. Success in improv demands that you ask your partner something specific enough to work with it but also can't refuse it.

Questions that ask why can be broad and open-ended and don't always work well in improv. However, "why" questions in business yield higher-order responses—those linked to strategic-level feedback. More on this a little later, but first, let's explore how curious and observant you are today.

Influencers

When you've had trouble answering it's usually because you've been asked the wrong question. Fix the question, not the answer.

Our curiosity manifests on multiple levels, and Million Dollar Influence requires that you fine-tune yours. It exists along a spectrum. Viktor Frankl in *Man's Search for Meaning*[2] promotes a deeply immersive connection to a positive state. Getting at the highly spiritual association of what life is about is a profound pursuit. While answering, "what will the weather be for the presentation tomorrow?" represents a far more superficial degree of curiosity. On which end of the curiosity spectrum are you closest?

See how the answer from a business counterpart might change if you substitute "why" for either "what" or "how" below:

- What power level do you require for the widget?
  - *Why do you need that power level?* It gives you a chance to participate in the understanding of the design.
- How will operators use the widget?
  - *Why do operators need to use the widget for that?* Provides an understanding of what the buyer is trying to accomplish.
- What is your buying timeline?
  - *Why is your buying timeline (so long or so short)?* You may be able to sell sooner or sell more if your supply supports it.
- How will you fund this acquisition?
  - *Why do you plan to fund the acquisition with a (buy vs. lease vs. license vs. cryptocurrency?).* It opens doors to creative financing options.
- What security protocols does the project require?
  - *Why is security not more fully integrated into this project?* It opens the discussion to unexamined risks.
- What credentials and experience must the new hire possess?
  - *Why do you need a new hire?* Identifies whether another problem exists and is more urgent.
- How does this capability improve efficiency?
  - *Why is efficiency the driving concern?* Efficiency might not be the best decision metric for the work of first responders, security officials, or warfighting, for example.

Keeping the word "why" at the ready can control almost any conversation. Your counterparts will have to think and defend their stated position. When you ask "why" in a thought-provoking, instead of aggressive manner, you gain credibility and likely more respect and time from your counterpart.

NOT ALL IMPROV IS READY FOR PRIME TIME

Saturday Night Live famously tweaks individual sketches up until the very last minute before airing and sometimes during the show's live broadcast. Some sketches don't draw laughs in front of a rehearsal audience hours before the live airing and don't survive. Dropping, adding, or modifying lines at the last minute or during the live show, can impact subsequent sketches. The sketches appearing later in the show that don't quite have the timing down or can't adapt to the new time allotment now won't fit into the live schedule as planned. Producers, under the direction of the show's long-time executive producer, Lorne Michaels, make the quick decision in the moment that the sketch will not air. Rather than force something that's not working out, they know to defer. They'll try the sketch another day, or it never gets used. Improv requires the timing and agility of the participants to succeed. You have to know when it's your time or adjust the conditions to create your time.

The ability to recognize when something won't work or is not working but could work later is equally essential. The meeting in Chapter 3 called for letting go of the script. Later in Chapter 6, we'll talk about penalties that correspond with misuse of time. Between throwing out the script and being penalized for delays, there is a middle ground where using the clock to your advantage makes sense. Football quarterbacks and coaches are experts at managing the clock in the final minutes of a close game. Scoring too soon in these cases can allow time for an opponent's comeback. They will control possession until the last seconds and score without leaving sufficient time for the opponent's response.

Some examples where letting the clock run can help are as follows:

- An impending change of political administration. Changes in law require political majorities; elections can change voting majorities.
- Diplomatic initiatives between nations; or doing business, or even attempting business, in a foreign nation.

- Planned or mandatory retirements of decision-making executives. Sometimes even short-term leaves of absence for health reasons can create a new opening.
- A reorganization of a team—this dynamic is ever-present in most large companies.
- Your technology has not sufficiently matured, but you fully expect it to work within a specific timeframe.
- Synchronizing business operations to industry activities such as trade shows and public messaging.
- Orchestrating communications plans such as ad campaigns or quarterly investor reporting.
- Rotation of decision-makers in government roles; most move every three years.

Tik-Tok star and voice of her generation, "Corporate Natalie," offers funny videos of phrases you may recognize. They can manifest as passive aggression in the wrong hands, but a skilled influencer knows how to use them to advantage and wait for a better time:

- The slow roll
- Letting it simmer
- Letting it marinate
- Putting a pin in it for now
- Circling back on that

"Keeping one's powder dry" is attributed to English statesman Oliver Cromwell circa 1650. Muskets must use dry gun powder to fire well. Being ready to fight another day is as important as being ready for your prime-time improv.

CHAPTER 4 SUMMARY

Improvisational comedy can be pretty funny, often because the degree of uncertainty for the audience heightens the anticipation of the moment. Those performing the improv are also subject to surprise along the way. However, the improvisation follows an order and moves with a flow that the audience isn't fully aware of. Examining how improvisation requires a fuller sense of the situation to succeed can broaden your perspective on business relationships.

Keeping the business dialogue positive allows it to move forward. Obstacles and perceived roadblocks are merely points of maneuver. Eliminating the negative associations of "no" allows for many more variations of "yes." You can consistently move toward yes when you're committed to an end-game beyond the immediate transaction.

Recognizing when the timing isn't right can keep you in the game. There are as many methods as logical reasons to defer a decision or an outcome. Repositioning a decision into a more favorable timeframe can often improve the odds of the win. As important as the concepts of improvisation are, forcing it can lead to a fast fail.

In Chapter 5, we'll identify ways in which you can identify the actual buyer and that there are buyers in any circumstance!

NOTES

1 *Infuence: The Psychology of Persuasion*, Harper Business, 2006.
2 Beacon Press, 1959.

5

The dynamics of the deal

The authority figure in a business deal can appear murky or even opaque when first approaching an opportunity. Chapter 2 illustrates that one can delegate authority but not accountability. The accountable individual may not be the decider. It may appear logical that the buyer is at the top of the organization chart; however, applying that logic would suggest the CEO does it all. You'll need to dig deeper.

A constellation of people surrounds the actual buyer in most decisions, planets circling the sun. In business decision mapping, there are gatekeepers, decision influencers, and decision enablers, each of whom can play a role in influencing a decision. Understanding the decision-making process can guide your moves, but the precision and efficacy of your language will carry the day. First, let's look at some organizations you're likely to encounter.

WHO'S ON FIRST?

Understanding the environment will aid in your success. Hierarchical organizations allow for top-down, centralized management and at least a perception of control by those at the top. In a hierarchical organization, functional leads such as marketing, sales, research, and R&D often report directly to the CEO or a COO. Most people you initially meet in B2B or B2G are looking up to a boss.

A leadership team typically confers about strategy and solutions among themselves and sometimes with board members, then sends the directions downward. Good governance requires a level of board engagement. However, an adjunct subcommittee of seniors often looks at a challenge

DOI: 10.4324/9781003320388-5

first, thereby diluting some accountability before the task(s) are sent downhill. In the wrong hands, a challenge worthy of quick action can fall victim to a committee intent on admiring the problem further.

Influencers

Teams always have a formal or informal leader, as do committees, as do boards, as do "executive councils." It's not necessarily "majority rule" but often "which way is the wind blowing for the leader."

Product leaders are an additional option to assign accountability. For example, within a hierarchy, Apple assigns product leaders for categories like services, Mac, or iPhone. Scrum management also uses product areas as lines of demarcation within a matrixed organization. Think of product organization horizontally, not vertically. Product organizations all tap into the shared functions listed above.

In many small businesses with annual revenues below $50 million and headcount below 500, the president (or founder) is most often the default final decision-maker. The organization chart may say one thing, but the informal power of the small business president will always be evident. Even with the delegation of authority, if proposing something new or outside the existing plan, the delegated authority in smaller businesses will prove inadequate.

In government settings such as federal agencies or even a congressional office, "ownership" of issues is typically defined by program, project, or portfolio—at least on paper. In government, the actual owner of the issue is the person or entity controlling the relevant line of the budget. It's etched in stone in government if something has no funding, it's not real. When you identify who can change budget allocations, you are closing in on where the power lies.

Influencers

The test for whether you have found the decision-maker is confirmation that they have both authority and means.

If you are a corporate executive or aspire to be one, you may recognize the power that accompanies control of funds in your immediate circle. You have a boss or bosses to whom you answer for tasking. But which of those people controls your paycheck? The person who determines whether your raise will be an additional .05% or 15% or whether you will receive a maximum or token bonus, or a "pink slip," is your real boss. Think about it.

Equally important in any organization is the informal power that flows in all directions. It may take any of several forms and stem from a variety of individuals:

- The person who invented a technology
- The rainmaker whose behavior is abhorrent but who brings in sales
- The boss's son or daughter, or anyone with the family name in a family business
- The person who is perceived to have a special relationship with a client or customer
- A former college roommate or friend
- A fellow veteran who may have served together with someone in authority
- A former government official who is now on the company payroll
- Any member of an "advisory committee" to the board or leadership
- In government, political appointees with particular allegiances (party, elected official, future aspirations)

Informal relationships can permeate any organization chart. Appreciating the impact of informal power on the organization will save you time and frustration. Applying Million Dollar Influence requires that you discern how the organization works.

GET YOUR HOUSE IN ORDER BEFORE ISOLATING THE ACTUAL BUYER

You may not notice that your actions are a part of a broader campaign that's continually unfolding. Your attire, demeanor, words, actions, and reputation continually represent you to the buying constellation. You may not yet recognize who the buyer is. You may not even acknowledge you're selling. *Million Dollar Influence is a form of selling.* While you are trying to identify who can make decisions, the people on the other side are sizing you up as well.

Influencers

Never "pitch" or even think about pitching, unless you're on the mound for a baseball team. Influence is about finding and appealing to the other person's self-interest. That self-interest may be professional, personal, or both.

Even if you are not engaged in a specific transaction of a good or service for a fee, you are selling yourself before you ever meet your counterpart(s). Everyone is selling. You're reading this book to improve your business acumen. By definition, you are in sales, and you need to get comfortable assessing where people fit into your buying constellation—just like they're assessing you.

In today's B2B and B2G world, digital identities matter. Part of your discovery of who the buyer is includes an online search. Websites, Google, and LinkedIn profiles can provide an incredible amount of information about any organization or individual with which and with whom you interact for business. Know that they each reflect the best version of that company or person and may not reflect the complete story.

Conversely, when you attempt to engage with the buying constellation, know that they are checking you out as well. Studies[1] demonstrate that 75% of buyers solve for themselves online, and nearly 50% of the buying decision occurs before the first live conversation between buyer and seller. What will they find when someone learns of you and conducts an online search? Further, buyers are four times more likely to trust the referral of a friend or colleague.[2]

This assessment of you by the audience with which you are trying to connect must be a critical element of your approach calculus. Having your digital presence in order is essential before you ask for an introduction, a referral, or make an overture requesting a meeting. Are you connecting appropriately before your first live interaction?

Use the model below to consider categorizing elements of the buying constellation when identifying where counterparts fit into an organization.

Gatekeepers, influencers, and enablers all have the power to say "no." *None of them has the power to say "yes."* Influencers and enablers can say "maybe," *but not "yes."* A few definitions before moving on are as follows:

- *Gatekeepers*: Schedulers, Executive Assistants, Personal Assistants. Schedulers can be a person or a digital scheduling tool. For example, a *de facto* gatekeeper is a tool that only shows availability on Tuesdays at 4 p.m.
- *Influencers*: The people the leaders and decision-makers respect, admire and who identify risk. To some influencers, everything can look risky, while others see new opportunities. They provide "light-bulb moments" for decision-makers and for colleagues.
- *Enablers*: the people who can do something positive to advance your position in the eyes of the decision-makers. They have the authority to set meetings, influence budget allocations, arrange for competitions, and so forth. Enablers have the trust of the decision-maker to take independent action to prepare a final decision. They won't decide but can help advance it pretty far toward final approval.

Influencers

Alan's enabler at Merck resulted in meeting over two dozen buyers and $2 million in business over 12 years, along with another $2 million in referrals from Merck.

In business and government, identification of the gatekeeper is a straight-forward exercise. Who answers the phone when you call the office? Who responds to your email inquiry? The gatekeeper is the outer perimeter to the inner circle.

In government, there is a cross-over animal known as the "confidential assistant." The job description highlights the confidential nature of the work, whether it's keeping the principals' secrets or dealing with the personal information of staff, such as pay. In business, one expects the executive assistant or secretary to keep things confidential in the office. However, the "confidential" title can add to one's self-importance in government. It's a badge of honor for some. Accept and work with it.

Knowing who's who is only helpful if you know how to apply that information to your situation. You'll need to be more thoughtful and masterful with your words when interacting with anyone in the buying constellation. Likely, you are not applying appropriate forethought to your engagement, spending too much time on process flow *and not enough time on content flow*. Up to now, we're focusing on processes such as organization charts and positioning. Next, we'll weave in the magic of words and show how they fit with your understanding of the process.

WORDS ARE BOTH SCIENTIFIC AND MAGICAL

Above, we focus on the stars of the buying constellation, and now it's time to make sure your words are up to the task. Alan writes in several books of the importance of delivering a message with energy, authority, and clarity. A recurring theme of success with words includes the use of appropriate vocabulary. Suppose you identify that Ms. Smith is the decision-maker, and you need to see her to demonstrate your capability or solution.

Here are some examples you might deploy with various people in support:

Speaking with a gatekeeper*: I know you can't confirm that Ms. Smith will be at the widget conference next week. But if I could get a sidebar with her for 10 minutes, it could save us from using your and her precious calendar time with a request for an office meeting. Her colleague, Bill Jones, made it clear you control the schedule and would be most helpful in connecting us. Can you put me together with Ms. Smith for lunch or at the conference reception?*

- You've applied tact, confirmed the gatekeeper's self-importance, and used flattery. You state you've spoken to a known colleague about the need for this meeting. Further, you're willing to go where it makes the most sense for the meeting.

Speaking with a decision influencer*: Nancy, I've admired your work for some time from a distance, not knowing we'd one day have a chance to work together potentially. I sense that Ms. Smith might not be getting the complete picture of what's available to help her. May I share an idea with you? Our work at ACME has allowed us to develop a unique and clever solution that we're finally ready to bring to market. I know the budget has already been approved, but I think you'll appreciate how a reallocation could better position the company in less than a year. Perhaps I could show you first in the coming days, and you could help elevate the discussion?*

- You acknowledge Nancy's perspective and ability to see beyond process. You make clear that Nancy could be the one who can bring something new and potentially game-changing into the decision orbit. You get her permission to proceed by asking, "May I?" It's not about you or your solution alone; you've planted something that allows Nancy to benefit as well.

Speaking with a decision enabler: *You know Tom, the USA Association should find a way to recognize Ms. Smith's work for the industry. What if the USA Association asked her to keynote at the trade show in June, or if we recognize her efforts with an award? Should a couple of us propose that idea and see if she'd be interested enough to attend in person?*

- You spoke to someone outside Ms. Smith's company, but whom Smith would recognize. Tom has influence in USA Association and the latitude to either create an award, bestow an award, or otherwise shape the programming at an industry trade show. You are creating a situation where you will further your relationship with Ms. Smith, garner public recognition, and set conditions for future dialogue. Tom at USA Association looks like a hero in the eyes of a valued senior member of the industry, Ms. Smith. You are moving chess pieces on the board.

In the situations above, it's not the words alone that make a difference.

The examples are admittedly simple; however, the construct you arrange with your words is subtle and sophisticated. You are being professional and giving without being obsequious or annoying. Most importantly, you understand who the players are and how they can be helpful. You are coupling two critical forms of flow we'll discuss next.

YOU REALLY CAN GO WITH THE FLOW

In identifying how to break down an organization chart and label the various decision-making participants, you can also see the associated flows that move through any organization. *All organizations rely on process flow and content flow.* Process flow requires appropriate language, relationships, and discussion. Content flow sequences date, time, and action.

Notice in the examples above how we weave each element of process flow and content flow into the conversations. It's not a checklist when done thoughtfully and professionally. The person on the other side of the conversation generally feels good about you because you recognize their importance in their part of the process.

When Gene works with companies that sell to the government, he finds that most are too anxious to get a meeting before they understand the flow. "I need you to help meet with Secretary Smith at the Department of Defense," for example. His response is always the same, "Why do you think Secretary Smith is your first stop?" Secretary Smith here is a euphemism for the most senior name they know about. Starting at the top without prior preparation is a fast track to failure.

The short-sighted thinking is costly in a number of ways:

- Speaking to the decision-maker, if it is Secretary Smith, before knowing the lay of the land will equate to a missed opportunity, and you won't get another shot at meeting Secretary Smith.
- In a meeting, Secretary Smith will want to know what's been done on the topic to this point. Why is your issue at the Secretary's level? Without good groundwork on your part, you'll be unable to respond effectively.
- Going straight to the decision-maker before clearly formulating your message or "ask" means you don't yet know what you need or want from Secretary Smith.

Taking the time to deliberately map your way through an organization before you land a meeting will strengthen your ultimate influence. Going with the flow instead of forcing your solution or suggestion on others will serve everyone well.

Influencers

You can gauge the flow of a river—speed, direction, depth, and so forth—by stepping into it. You don't drown when you step off the bank, but you can drown if you jump into the middle without knowing these dynamics.

Some examples of flow you should find familiar, and you could be using to your advantage are listed below. Notice how some can also be a fulcrum for the lever from Chapter 3:

- Program reviews (monthly and quarterly)
- Timecard and expense approvals

- Milestone decision meetings
- Any business travel
- Board meetings of any type
- Industry trade show schedules
- In government, any form of "review," such as quadrennial, annual, milestone, presidential, or Congressional
- Budget formulation, to include all levels of defending budget requests
- Retirements and planned personnel rotations and promotions
- Performance reviews
- Changes in political administrations or party control

CHAPTER 5 SUMMARY

Deals don't have checklists. It doesn't matter what the deal is—a meeting, a sale, an effort to change policy—deals are more about nuance and movement. Normal pressures can cause you to "feel the need for speed," as Tom Cruise famously declares in the original movie, *Top Gun*. However, speed can also kill deals when not well-controlled.

We've described the value of understanding the playing field on which you and your counterparts live and work. Just like mapping criminal or terrorist organizations, when you understand the organization chart and the concept of flow, you'll be in a better position to align your influence for maximum effect.

Most jobs would be easy if it weren't for the people! Alan identifies the "great resignation" of the pandemic as really "the existential jailbreak!"[3] Many people are unhappy in their current roles and paralyzed to change their circumstances. In Chapter 6, we'll show you how to identify challenging human behaviors that are part of the influence terrain.

NOTES

1 CSO Insights annually publishes its Sales Enablement Pro drawn from global sales survey data.
2 See Nielsen's annual Global Survey of Trust in Advertising.

3 As we write this, unemployment is at 3.8%, which is virtually zero, according to economists who dismiss the chronically unemployed. The "great resignation" also resulted in the "great reemployment."

6

Delay of game penalties

In the "best companies to work for," identified on various annual lists[1], personnel dynamics and human resource conformance consume the office energy. Sadly, many executives spend over half of their time on internal issues having nothing to do with revenue generation, identifying opportunities, or moving the company toward a place of advantage. Taken collectively, meetings without focus, quarterly reviews, program updates, performance reviews, compensation modeling, disciplinary issues, and more dominate calendars and inhibit a clear understanding of the actual playing field. This clutter clouds the view of critical ingredients of influence.

In Figure 6.1, you can estimate what percentage of your organization's talent and energy is directed toward your product, service, and/or relationships, and what percentage is eroded internally. The best organizations are 10% internal and 90% external, though many reverse that! (Just announce a layoff and see what happens.)

TOO MANY PLAYERS ON THE FIELD

In Chapter 5, we identify what Alan calls the "existential jailbreak." When the external pressure of the COVID-19 pandemic forced people to confront their mortality differently, many looked around at their circumstances and didn't like what they saw.

Some recognized their choices were not their own or the ones they would choose going forward. They were compromising with their work's fulfillment, bosses, and teammates in their orbit, as well as prospects for growth. The pandemic clarified where changing jobs, professions, or geographic locations vividly made sense. The *Harvard Business Review*[2] published

DOI: 10.4324/9781003320388-6

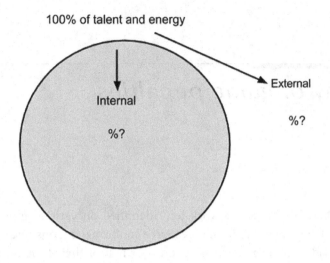

FIGURE 6.1
Where are your talent and energy being directed?

findings of a study of 4,000 companies identifying the 30–45-year-old age group as the most on the move. With 10–20 years in the workforce, this cohort in the trenches wants something more.

Influencers

If most of their recognition, satisfaction, and sense of achievement are accomplished outside of work, why would anyone choose to stay in such work if they were able to leave it?

Despite the changes in the workforce, employees not on salary find that they can't consistently be granted forty hours of weekly work. As a result, they don't qualify for health or retirement benefits and are sometimes forced to look for additional work—a side business or a second job. Why isn't there enough work to fully employ the hires? Is it a lack of work? Poor hiring practices? Or, is it simply less expensive to have more employees who won't qualify for costly benefits?

Whether salaried or hourly, many companies are over-staffed. Three themes are identifiable in the jailbreak's root causes:

1. Narrow roles and responsibilities create a perceived need to have specialized personnel filling too many positions.

2. Poor division of authority inhibits real accountabilities.
3. A crowded workforce in an organization makes for a pyramid with a very wide bottom and bottleneck top, so there's no upward mobility.

Government agencies are not immune to the bloat with more "billets" (in government parlance) than necessary, each identified with a verbose and overly complex job description. Go to the USAJobs[3] website, and you'll get an idea of the bureaucracy that cloaks federal hiring practices. To assure equitable hiring and satisfy well-intended diversity goals, we see a process that's the antithesis of an entrepreneurial or "disruptive" spirit.

Working for a government agency is safe. It is pretty difficult to fire a government employee short of committing an egregious or unlawful act (as it is in higher education, political appointments, law enforcement, and much of the media). Concern over failure to ensure due process for the individual in a government termination process makes the hiring process more challenging. Government agency hiring is purposely difficult as agencies take extra steps to prevent what may be a bad hire.

As a business executive approaching organizations to influence your preferred outcome, you'll need to consider these undercurrents that run through all organizations. In describing this condition, we aim to sensitize you to this genuine layer of confusion you must permeate to create real influence. Your empathy for the individuals who live under the weight of these organizational pressures can be helpful.

We call the miscommunications and misunderstandings that can occur "the thermal layer," depicted in Figure 6.2. This is the stratum where communications and understanding, with the best of intentions, are "refracted" in unintended directions.

Like submarine warfare, submarines can hide below a thermal layer. Aircraft and ships attempting to locate a submarine must understand the effects of the thermal layer and either coordinate sonar energy appropriately or place a sensor below the thermal layer. Leadership must know what's happening below the thermal layer and to do so, must use methods to penetrate it.

Most employees who have been in the workforce, whether in business or government, for more than five years know the informal rules of their organization. They understand how to get into the fast lane and circumvent internal bureaucracy. When attempting to influence government outcomes, former agency employees are often great business hires. The revolving door of the more senior levels of government, where appointees spend

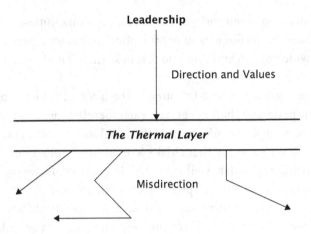

FIGURE 6.2
The thermal layer

a few years in a position then move to industry for double or triple the government salary, is alive and well. The industry is happy to pay the salary premium for insider knowledge of how an agency operates.

FALSE STARTS

False starts in football are known as "dead ball" fouls before the ball is in motion. A player on the offensive line of scrimmage moves, giving the appearance of the play in motion. The ball is dead when the referee signals the penalty, and the offense is penalized five yards. It wastes time and energy in the game.

With the confusion one can face identifying the real "players" of an organization and the circuitous content and process flow that accompany the reality of the crowded field, you will inevitably allow dialogue with the wrong player to create a false start. Such false starts in business waste your time, so identifying a possible and potential false start quickly is essential.

False starts aren't limited to sales engagements. They can manifest within hierarchies, across teams, and the continuous processes that sustain bureaucracies. Alan uses the term "failure work" to describe doing something more than once that did not get done right the first time (see illustration 6.1 above: Failure work is within the circle, not focused on customers and products). False starts create failure work. Do you recognize any of these false starts?

- Pre-screening as a vendor within a supply chain
  - *While necessary for due diligence, you can get buried in this process*
- "Thanks for coming in. We aren't ready right now, but we will keep you in our active file."
  - *This is a clear refusal without using the word "no"*
- Being diverted to a small business online entry portal
  - *Default to process as opposed to you being pulled through the system and into a conversation*
- Beginning a dialogue with a program manager who rotates out within months causes you to have to begin a new relationship
  - *This often happens in government and can be avoided by including others in the conversation early*
- A senior officer takes your meeting and hands you off to a subordinate who specializes in your area
  - *Settling for this without a clear timeline to follow up with the senior will create failure work*
- Negotiating pricing with a "buyer" with no authority to buy
  - *Developing a sense of who really owns the checkbook is essential*
- The award of a five- or six-figure small business innovation research (SBIR) contract in government
  - *In the government, single-digit millions are pencil dust. SBIR contracts are a form of seed corn, not "program of record" dollars that can improve your revenue*
- "Let's get together when you're in town next."
  - *A vague reference to an unspecified future date*
- "Here's my card, call my assistant, and we'll set something up."
  - *"I'm too important to run my calendar." You have not gotten through yet, but you think you have.*

OFFSIDES AND PERSONAL FOULS

Influencer

People want to work with likable people and people they like!

The reciprocity of The Golden Rule, treating others as you would like to be treated, remains sage counsel in any situation. It's such easy a guideline to follow and will help you generate influence. The Golden Rule is about being thoughtful.

As with moving in too fast before identifying and understanding the organizational landscape, rushing a personal engagement can have the same negative result. Consistently putting yourself in your counterpart's shoes will help you develop a positive pattern of behavior and a reputation as a thoughtful and agreeable person. You don't need to be obsequious, just thoughtful and sensitive.

Influence requires relationships, and relationships require consideration more so than equity. Meeting your counterpart 60/40 instead of meeting halfway or going for the "win" will garner outsized returns for the effort. Generating more, even if smaller, wins for your counterpart will yield more wins for you as well. *Not every engagement is a transaction, and you don't have to squeeze the last drop out of every engagement.*

Nobody wants to spend time with someone who is boorish or inconsiderate. We can often recognize someone else's poor manners but can fail to see our transgressions through the eyes of others. Could any of these subtle acts of selfishness be bleeding over into your business relationships?

- Running red lights or coasting through four-way stops
  - *Focus on you*
- Speaking first in a group setting
  - *You know the answer or know more*
- Assumptions of all types
- Thinking you are the smartest in the room
  - *It's less likely than you think*
- Making negative comments on social media
- Talking "over" people
- Filling moments of silence where room for thought may be appropriate
- Failing to read the room
- Missing social cues
- Taking what is a premium seat in a group setting
- Failing to include a new person into a conversation or group business activity
  - *How often do you see the same posse of old-timers congregating at trade shows for your industry?*

- Displays of what Alan calls "moral narcissism" where you declare, "I'm right, and you're not only wrong, but inferior."

The common thread that runs through the list above is selfishness. Some expressions of thoughtfulness that cost you nothing are as follows:

- A thank you note—for anything—will always be appreciated
  - *And will distinguish you from the masses in any organization, especially if hand-written*
- Not calling or stopping by your counterpart out of the blue
  - *Cold-calling someone says your time is more valuable than theirs; scheduling demonstrates respect and increases the focus of the encounter.*
- Being early for your scheduled visit
  - *If your counterpart is running early, you can keep them running early*
  - *Early is on time; on time is late—but don't overdo it*
- Not overstaying your scheduled visit
  - *Giving time back on someone's calendar helps them*
- Not introducing a surprise issue into a meeting arranged for another purpose
- Asking about your counterpart without invading their personal space
  - *Some cultures view "biographical" questions as intrusive unless they initiate the discussion*
- Birthday cards for people you know are always welcome
- Holding doors open for others
- Asking for input from others
- Engaging with office staff, wait staff, and service personnel
  - *Simple courtesy and acknowledgment go a long way*
- Offering to make the arrangements when there is an agreement to meet or dine
- Picking up the tab if you initiated the meeting; offering to share a tab where you are a guest
- Waiting for a host to begin eating before you dive into a meal
- Saying thank you, making direct eye contact when doing so

- Forwarding *relevant* professional materials that may be of interest to a business colleague
  - *Meaningful additive comments should accompany such a gesture*
- Giving credit to all contributors
- Summarizing a meeting with a timely and courteous follow-up thank you email
- Don't assume you know what roles people are there to serve
  - *Treat everyone in the room as equals*

Case Study: The Ferrari

Alan had to visit his client, Mercedes Benz, about three hours away, so he took his Ferrari to give it a good run on the interstate. He arrived 30 minutes early, as planned, and parked in the visitor's space in front of the all-glass lobby.

When he walked in, an executive vice president whom he had never met said, "Is that car yours?" When Alan acknowledged it was, the executive said, "I have two of them, can you stop by my office after your appointment and we can chat?"

Alan made a new contact, had a new buyer, and that's because he arrived early and was an object of interest to a powerful person.

THE GRANDSTANDING OF OFFICE POLITICS

Throughout *Million Dollar Influence*, we identify formal and informal organizational structures and hierarchies. The corrosiveness of office politics can weaken the effectiveness of those organizations. Such behaviors manifest in multiple forms: passive-aggressive responses, gossip, lying, taking credit for others' work, withholding information, or failure to support a colleague in need, for example. *Office politics are about power at the expense of others.*

Like pseudo-charismatic leadership, where the leader uses personal charisma to exert influence to support a narcissist need, office politics co-opt progress and inhibit positive outcomes. Whether you are inside an organization or approaching one from the outside, identifying the negative behavior for what it is will save time. Influence can survive regardless but requires an elevated perspective to do so.

Influencers

Most people simply bemoan office politics as if it's like the weather—unavoidable. But that's a misconception.

(About the politics, not the weather.)

When applying influence, by definition, you threaten the status quo. The threat of disruption to the "order" means power may shift and inspire some of the behaviors above as incumbents cling to their roles. You can arrest office politics by confronting it directly and promoting communication pathways that limit the conditions that allow such corrosion in the first place.

Office politics exist because it's tolerated at some level. Stemming it requires confronting it directly. Influencers don't shy away from calling out destructive behaviors. Internal communication channels exist for protest or debate, but carry the baggage of human resources in their use. Does HR serve the employee or the company?

The incorporation of transparent software collaboration tools such as channels, boards, and chats serve an important secondary function beyond their ability to replace email and point-to-point communications such as the telephone. Collaboration tools force people out of the shadows and publicly communicate their ideas. Business communication tools will continue to change as email and telephone communications wane, and the metaverse evolves. And they can be highly effective even remotely.

Today, many in the workforce only know of a business world with email communication. Those fewer and fewer older workers who pre-date email knew both the power and pitfalls of informal and point-to-point communication where idle chatter can thrive. Younger workers who grew up with online multiplayer gaming, and the "Discord"[4] app it inspired, readily embrace the open communication tools now emerging in the workplace. While older workers may reach for the instruction manual that no longer exists in paper form, younger workers readily embrace the latest channels and boards and figure out the nuances.

When those who engage in office politics must work in a genuinely transparent environment, their poor behaviors are on full display and more readily eradicated. Just as you learn on the playground that standing up to a bully changes the bully's behavior, the same applies in business communications. *But is it a single bully, or could it be a corrosive culture?*

THE POLITICAL LANDSCAPE

Recall from Chapter 1 that culture links beliefs with behaviors. An undercurrent of culture is the political landscape of an organization. What actions does the organization support, encourage or tolerate? These are often unwritten. Think of it as an intrinsic code that you won't find on a hallway or break room poster.

Like culture, the impact of an organization's political landscape flows from the top, be it a charismatic president, a leadership team of C-suite executives, a political appointee, or a career civil servant. Have you ever heard the saying, "What interests my boss fascinates me?" The converse is, "Mrs. Jones won't support that; don't even bring it up in the meeting." Both reflect a political landscape.

Some examples that dot a political landscape are as follows:

- Everyone gets an annual raise as opposed to merit-based raises
- Liberal interpretation of travel and expense rules
- Titles imply authority people don't have
- Excessive use of personal time off (PTO) inhibits the content flow
- Support of particular charities, associations, or candidates
- Failure to discipline personnel violations of some people
- Tolerance of abrasive behaviors of some people
- No remote work because the boss wants "butts in seats," reflecting poor trust
- Support of a political candidate
  - *It is illegal to direct support of a political candidate in any form*

Except for supporting political candidates, the list contains what become informal policies and practices. Some aspects of a political landscape reveal insidious ways that people may overlook or choose not to care about something. Most often, the political landscape reveals what people go along with.

Case Study

During a client training session on strategy and leadership, Gene asked the assembly via a live poll using Mentimeter[5] to name three sources of their news. Responses were tilted very noticeably toward extreme right-wing cable TV and radio channels and included names of conservative pundits. Not surprisingly, the company president routinely spoke openly in meetings about his faith, support for President Trump, and disdain for the ills of the Democratic Party.

Employees couldn't notice until confronted with the evidence of an anonymous poll how strongly this narrow input of information would reinforce their own biases. In this case, those customer-facing employees were unaware of the degree to which they were carrying the beliefs of the boss into their business conversations.

As with office politics, unhealthy behaviors can spread like weeds. Wanting to be included, people adapt their behaviors so as not to stand out negatively. "Groupthink" confirms people will go along with a position when it is perceived as the consensus response of the group, even when they don't personally agree. Million Dollar Influencers readily recognize these organizational idiosyncrasies and weaknesses.

CHAPTER 6 SUMMARY

Any business engagement could be much simpler if it weren't for some of the people involved! However, our reality is that influence requires us to maneuver amidst people.

Whether they are unwilling or unable to see your desired objective or are simply uninformed, Million Dollar Influence *requires that you acknowledge and act* to align people's actions with your desired outcomes.

Understanding people's behaviors in decision-making within organizations is the first step toward overcoming those that may otherwise inhibit your influence. Million Dollar Influence requires that you take action regardless of the environment at the appropriate points. In Chapter 7, we'll learn from the Aztecs and see how to stake out terrain and maneuver with confidence.

NOTES

1 Glassdoor and Inc. Magazine are examples of private enterprises that survey the work-forces of small, medium, and large companies. Partnership for Public Service surveys government agencies. Data are compiled in lists with rankings or color-coding for each survey and accompanied by representative quotes from survey participants.
2 See https://hbr.org/2021/09/who-is-driving-the-great-resignation.
3 See https://www.usajobs.gov/?c=opportunities.
4 Discord is now used by tens of millions of people aged 13 and above. Its origins trace to a community chat feature popular in online gaming.
5 Mentimeter is an online polling tool allowing for real-time anonymous surveys with responses entered through mobile devices.

7

Stakeholders and stakes in the ground

Million Dollar Influencers understand influence doesn't mean pleasing everyone. While we may all be equal as human beings, not everyone has a stake in the outcomes in the business of influence. Some will resist change for the sake of resisting change. They lack imagination or let fear's hold immobilize them. Recognizing actual stakeholders will guide your positioning of stakes in the ground that will mark critical positions leading to your desired outcome.

WHAT THE AZTECS INTENDED

The Aztec empire grew and ruled for roughly two centuries beginning circa 1350 and was the dominant force of Mesoamerica. Their success is attributed to the formation of alliances and through the application of warfare. Conquests would pay tribute to retain loose control by local leaders. The Aztecs did not seek domination; they sought control.

The Aztec empire brought significant discoveries such as chocolate from the cacao plant, knowledge of medicine, and the uses of mathematics. However, Aztecs are perhaps best known for their use of human sacrifices to demonstrate class stratification between the Aztecs and their newly conquered subjects. They did not rely on the need to kill their opponent. Instead, they preferred to capture and subsequently control.

The Aztecs were applying a specific method, a manifestation of influence in its crudest and most brutal form. The point is not that one must use force to garner a win. Aztec influence grew considerably from the

DOI: 10.4324/9781003320388-7

implementation of a well-understood model. Confidence in one's model or plan is essential.

The Aztecs were the source of the phrase "to put a stake in the ground." They fought with ankles tethered to the stake where they would either be victorious or die. They did not retreat. (Of course, it was difficult to pursue vanquished opponents when staked to one spot, a very tactical shortcoming.)

IDENTIFYING THE KEY PLAYERS

We helped you understand organizational dynamics in the preceding chapters that you may not have paid sufficient attention to heretofore. We also identified players who manifest key behaviors in any organization: decision-makers, buyers, influencers, enablers, and gatekeepers. You can act faster and more confidently when you have a model in mind that helps you sort and put order to what you observe. You can also ignore a lot of the noise and stop wasting energy!

Many people are addicted to being liked. Hence, "likes" on social media are a sign of prestige. However, many people act too timidly in new settings out of an irrational fear of what others may think and a fear that they will not be liked. The fear reveals a lack of confidence. When lacking confidence, some people default to a posture of deference and subordination. Courtesy is always appropriate, as we'll discuss, but once you identify key players, you'll recognize that *the opinions of many have no bearing on your desired outcomes*. When you embrace this reality, you can focus your business-related energy on the people who matter most.

Influencers

Respect is far more important than affection.

Note the subtlety here. It's not that some people don't matter. Of course, people matter, and they each deserve the respect due any individual. But their actions and opinions don't matter to your desired outcomes. You won't win everybody over, and you don't need to. *You're working to win the right people over.*

Applying your organizational knowledge to your specific business situation can amplify your confidence to move more boldly. The Aztecs above sought to dominate their environment and identifiable foes, but they did not see the need to kill their enemy every time. They walked confidently because they were exercising a plan that they knew would work. Million Dollar Influence is helping you formulate your model of what you want to unfold in any given setting.

OOZING CHARM

We all know when someone commands a room. One exudes a certain charisma when in command of a room. Smiles and stories come quickly, and conversations seem effortless as small audiences gather around and strain to hear. The military term for this collective attribute is "command presence." An individual has it or doesn't—but can get it. Command presence can apply to any business encounter as easily as it applies to senior military officials, celebrities, and politicians.

Most of us can develop command presence and exude confidence when we learn how to turn on some charm. Being charming equates to being pleasant and outgoing. Even the self-described introvert can learn when to turn up personal energy.

Influencers

"Command" implies "authority" and all the responsibility attendant to it.

Similarly, "retail politicians" with a knack for remembering names, kissing babies, and offering compliments know how to be on for the moment even when they might not feel like it. Personal energy can lift others around them to higher spirits and purpose. People of all walks like to associate with confident and successful people who live in a positive frame of mind. Command presence is a learnable skill that can be amplified or muted as appropriate to the situation.

Many politicians who rise to the most senior government positions are skilled wearing the "mask of command," knowing when to dial the charm up or down. Ronald Reagan was an actor long before he became President of the United States. He understood presence and "showtime" as few others. Similarly, Bill Clinton has a gift of making the most uncomfortable person in a room full of people feel noticed and included.

Being charming is about expressing interest in the other person and breaking invisible barriers. How many conferences or networking receptions have you attended where new people uncomfortably sought the perceived safety of other new people (or the buffet line)? More often than not, they divert to the bar to occupy themselves, effectively looking busy. How often do you see the same tired warhorses traveling in packs or cliques at industry events?

Commanding a room requires one to be completely present at the moment. It also requires adherence to a few well-understood rules of dress and etiquette. Looking the part matters. The overarching inhibition that prevents people from commanding a room is a needless concern about what to say, when to say it, and to whom to say it.

Let's test your command presence. Do you do any of these things regularly?

- When entering a reception, you immediately proceed to the bar
  Stop at the first person you encounter, introduce yourself and ask where they're from and what they hope to achieve at the reception. You can then offer to refresh a drink or proceed to the bar together—even better, to meet more people.
- When participating in a meeting, you greet each person in the room personally before getting down to business
  This common courtesy applies to everyone, men and women. You can set your things down at a seat, but making this simple gesture commands attention because many don't do it.
- You attempt to meet new people at conferences
  Entering a situation with purpose changes your demeanor, even if you set a simple goal to meet a handful of new people—not a quick card or e-card exchange, but a genuine connection. Don't be aloof; engage confidently. And try to meet people who seem uncomfortable or hesitant to join conversations. (This is Bill Clinton's great knack to create comfort in others.)
- You arrange dinners with a familiar group at conferences more than two times per year
  While it's fun to meet with old friends, being the social coordinator is not improving your influence, and it can make you appear unapproachable to others

- You consciously select your wardrobe for a particular event
  You must make an effort; sharp dress gets noticed. Not extreme or eccentric, sharp! This applies to men and women alike. Think of it as an identity; it has to be accurate.
- You review news *from credible sources* daily
  This simple act provides fuel for conversations. People who are uncomfortable in new settings believe they don't know what to say. Commenting on or asking a question about topical news is an easy icebreaker for both parties.

Case Study: The truckers

Alan was at a cocktail reception for the board of a hospital before speaking at their event. He was introduced to the CEO of the largest trucking firm in the state and the eighth largest in the USA. He immediately asked, "What are the implications for you of Consolidated Freight declaring bankruptcy?" (they were the largest US carrier. The CEO spoke for 20 minutes without stopping).

- In a meeting when approaching a decision point, do you press for a decision, recap the scenario up to the moment, or suggest a follow-up?
  Any option could be appropriate, and knowing when to choose one over the others doesn't have to be complicated. It's the hesitation to choose one at the moment that gives away your influence. Leading the other party to the appropriate option commands influence.
- Offering of compliments
  This applies to ideas brought by others, arrangements someone made, parameters proposed, suggestions of terms in a deal, or an outline of a way ahead. Some examples are as follows:

  "Bob, your idea to try and close early could really work for us. What might get in the way that we could address now?"

  "Judy, including all that you've suggested might be a stretch for some others. How can we work together to associate each parameter with a mutually agreeable timeline?"

  "We certainly have a good problem to resolve because we have many good ideas to choose from. If we build on what Cindy is charting as a way ahead, we can move this along much faster than we all might have originally thought."

- Do you use "yes, but…" in any form?
  The word "but" has become a code for a micro-aggression. An alternative to the implied rejection of "but" is to reframe. An example would be "Bill, if we use that methodology, what do those next two or three steps look like?" as opposed to, "Yes, Bill, but what about the aggressive timeline?"
  Let the individual who proposed an idea you don't like work through the next steps more publicly. They will often catch themselves in mid-sentence and backtrack while thinking out loud. You are applying influence without even speaking.
  "Dr. Scott, I understand your initial plan, but what happens in the weeks following and who's accountable?"
- Do you establish clear lines of progression, demarcation, or decision?
  When you are the one suggesting a way to frame and decide a problem or opportunity, you are exerting influence. Note this does not need to be done forcefully. You don't need "red lines"; you want an identifiable and mutually agreeable way forward.

Alan writes extensively that mastery of language is critical to any business encounter. It's okay and is reasonable to consider some rehearsal before the encounters. The preparation for the encounters helps those short on natural charisma to perfect their mask of command.

Oozing charm and charisma comes naturally to some. Unfortunately, many charismatic people cannot read the room and are overbearing in the eyes of others. Be honest with your self-assessment of how well you prepare for the known knowns of any meeting. There's a big difference between Bill Clinton making people comfortable and a snake oil salesman pitching magic potions.

_____

HERDING CATS OR HERDING SHEEP?

Influencing is herding. For centuries, shepherds have understood how to single-handedly move a sometimes-disorganized flock to pasture, shearing, or market. Not all methods of herding work the same way.

Herding cats is a perfect metaphor for the application of influencing people for three reasons. First, cats act on their own time when they are ready. (Have you encountered the "not invented here" syndrome?) Whether a cat decides to pursue a mouse, lounge in the sun, or accept your stroking its head, cats are notoriously prickly to engage. Second, cats don't need your permission to live their lives. It's not just that they can't speak; they have no attachment to what you think. (Do you encounter people who are merely working to live as opposed to living to work?) And third, a group of independent-minded cats can only be guided from behind to move in a generally forward direction. Even incentivizing them with food from the front of the pack won't capture the attention of all of the cats. The metaphor conjures an image of a loosely organized pack of cats grudgingly responding to a master's instruction or prodding. You won't please everyone or win everyone over—stop trying to do so.

Have you ever observed a German Shepherd (which is included in breeds known as "working dogs") responding to its human companion while working? Humans and dogs function as one when moving livestock from place to place. The dogs can also work with other dogs, still responding to one master. Sheep, lambs, goats, horses, and cattle all respond to the dog's movement. Quick sharp whistles instruct the dogs to perform a specific task to herd the obedient livestock. The dogs are very fast, very responsive, and highly engaged. They live for the excitement of the work. In response to the dogs' movements, the herd moves in near-perfect unison where the master's orders take it. The key here is the dog and master have rehearsed this skill and then honed it through repetition to apply it in myriad scenarios. The result is masterful in its efficiency.

Allow yourself the freedom to think of the people in your circles of influence as needing some "herding" and consider the parallels. Even a highly skilled person with a German Shepherd can't herd cats.

SUCCESS, NOT PERFECTION: RECOGNIZING THE SUFFICIENT "WIN"

You can be right and even prove yourself right, or you can achieve your objective. Which do you want? Which matters most? We suggest it's far more essential to achieve your objective than to chase the concept of being proven right. Influence is not only about winning; you want to be able to repeat it consistently. More on this in Chapter 10, but for now, we're trying to keep bridges in place, improve connections, and move toward mutually agreeable outcomes that are good enough—success, not perfection.

Influencers

He was right, dead right, as he hurtled into traffic without looking, knowing that he had the right-of-way. But once he was hit by the beer truck, he was just as dead as if he'd been dead wrong.

Being competitive can be a response to the adrenalin of a situation and can be healthy; however, it can also cloud your perspective at the moment. Fearing you are losing ground, running out of time, or about to fail to close a deal, you risk acting more aggressively or abruptly than is appropriate (or effective).

Very few business encounters require the intensity of a Super Bowl or Olympic final. You can influence more business encounters by approaching them with the intensity of a half-court basketball scrimmage. You come together to work toward a mutually agreeable outcome, and as in scrimmage basketball, you'd like to return to do it again.

Even in the most high-profile, cut-throat competitions, such as The United States v. Microsoft anti-trust suit that dragged on for years, there will be another day. Similarly, the defense department's $10 billion dollar Joint Enterprise Defense Infrastructure (JEDI) was a "winner-take-all" endeavor contested for years. Amazon and Microsoft fought hammer-and-nail for the win, each exerting enormous capital only to see the contract opportunity canceled. *Yet there were multiple ways in which multiple winners could have come about.* However, each contractor presented itself to the government customer as the only solution. Each failed to influence because they let the competition bring about destructive behaviors worthy of credible protests.

Influencing is not winning; it is getting to your preferred outcome as efficiently as possible. Efficiency in this context means reasonable investments in time, resources, and relationship engagement. You don't need to bring a flamethrower to a business discussion. Scorching your counterpart means you'll likely never do business again and someone's going to call the cops.

You don't need to lay down lines in the sand, and there are no hills to die on in business. You won't win everyone over and should stop even trying. Similarly, you won't get everything you ask. That is fine. When you walk more confidently into each new situation, you'll begin to see patterns and more quickly identify which techniques will fit best.

The overarching success will manifest in how well you are perceived as you reach more of your preferred outcomes.

CHAPTER 7 SUMMARY

We highlight the Aztecs as one group which successfully exercised influence by deploying a model focused on expansion, not absolute dominance. They won the right people over as they confidently grew their empire. The Aztecs would allow the wins for others at the local levels, letting local leaders lead because they were not consequential to the more significant outcome the Aztecs were pursuing—expansion. And they never retreated.

In Chapter 8, we'll get you into the fast lane, where you'll move to unconscious competence in these and other skills. You'll begin to see that the conscious competence of preparing for encounters will allow you to move faster and exert Million Dollar Influence more routinely—even by default.

8

Acceleration

Urban planners think about car-driving habits through conscious competence. They have specific expertise that is thoughtfully applied to consider the myriad ways you might drive your car around town, between cities, or to the dreaded office building. Traffic flows best when all the design features work as intended: the high occupancy vehicle (HOV) lane, merging lanes, traffic lights, turn signals, and speed postings.

On the other hand, racecar drivers perfect their driving skills to the point of unconscious competence. They see openings several cars ahead. What may appear to the novice as imperceptible movements of the steering wheel can shift the car to an even more perfect line on the track. A spotter speaks into the driver's ear via radio to signal slow-downs or opportunities ahead. Their intense focus on the driver and team allows a near-complete integration of the driver and car. Your focus on the right things and rehearsing and instantiating them to the point of unconscious competence will speed your rate of Million Dollar Influence.

THE HOV LANE OR AN E-Z PASS?

HOV lanes were introduced in the United States in the 1970s to promote ride-sharing during the energy crisis of the day. Lanes designating special access for cars carrying two (HOV-2), three (HOV-3), or more passengers allow passage around areas of heaviest traffic congestion. Cities with the worst driving commutes, such as New York, Washington, DC, and Newark, New Jersey, evolved the concept of High Occupancy Toll (HOT) lanes.

HOV and HOT lanes may or may not solve the overall transportation problems as many cities with such lanes still report low usage of the public

DOI: 10.4324/9781003320388-8

transportation alternatives such as buses and rail. *Make way for the E-Z Pass lanes!* They are an even more deliberate way to bypass the congestion associated with the commuting masses. With flexible toll pricing, drivers with an E-Z Pass can choose whether or not they'll use the faster lane to bypass congestion by paying the traffic-sensitive price. You buy the E-Z Pass, and the overhead reader charges your account as your car passes through. Is it sometimes worth $35 or $50 flexible toll to bypass a problem? For Million Dollar Influencers, the answer is yes.

Cast Study: The HOV lane

Alan was picked up at LAX to go to a speech by a woman who volunteered to do so. She drove onto "the" 405 (California highways are always preceded by "the" as opposed to the East, where we just say "I95.") The road was a parking lot, with cars moving under 20 miles per hour.

Alan pointed to the extreme left lane which was moving at about 50 MPH. "Why don't you move over there?" he asked his driver.

"I can't," she explained, "it's for high occupancy vehicles."

"What constituted 'high occupancy,'" Alan asked.

"Two or more people," she said.

After a few seconds, Alan asked, "Which one of us isn't here?"

We seem to become stuck in our habits, not realizing when we can move faster and more efficiently.

You can move more efficiently through any organization or business encounter by using the equivalent of an E-Z Pass. Sometimes you need to pay a small premium to improve your situation. Consider such premiums in business to be equivalent to your E-Z Pass. Let's look at some examples of E-Z Passes you need to re-consider and may be completely overlooking right in front of you. You may think you still don't deserve to be in that lane.

You must be hyper-efficient with your time and the time you request of others. Scheduling and diligently managing time underpins everything Million Dollar Influencers do. Respecting your time and that of your counterpart helps every undertaking move faster. Nearly as important, when you respect other people's time, you strengthen their respect for you. You'll have an easier time getting follow-on meetings, sales, and business opportunities.

Influencers

You can always make another dollar but you can never make another minute.

When moving in political circles, campaign contributions[1] *for elected officials make a difference.* How often have you heard someone say something like, "I know Congressman Butler"? The operative question is, "Does Congressman Butler know you?" If you're a contributor to the Congressman's campaign, the odds that he knows you improve considerably. Your being known moves things along. Don't think of it as "pay-to-play" when your contribution supports someone else's desire to serve. We may not like the fact that campaigns cost money, but they do. Get used to it.

Become a member of multiple professional clubs. The ability to meet with people privately in a comfortable setting where you are known conveys stature. It signifies that your business engagements are important. It's a different meeting than you'll have at any "fast-casual" restaurant surrounded by families and kids! Your subtle control of the setting will focus your meetings while giving you an edge.

Maintain active membership in professional associations in your industry. You catch more fish when you fish where the fish are! Simple as that. Memberships allow you to absorb the material your counterparts absorb, like newsletter readings, association magazines (digital and print), or panels and keynotes at conventions. Doing so keeps you attuned to industry issues that matter to potential buyers and partners. Leadership roles in the more prominent associations will afford you uncommon access to industry and government. When you represent issues above and beyond your own and represent hundreds or thousands of companies and people, your voice carries additional authority.

Case Study: The car keys

A man came upon a friend searching in the street.
"Did you lose something?" he asked.
"Yes, my car keys," responded his friend.
"And you lost them right here?"
"No, I dropped them outside the restaurant up the street."
"Then why are you looking for them here?"
"Because the light is better here."

Make it a habit to write thank-you notes. They will never go out of style. A hand-written thank-you note on high-quality, personalized stationery differentiates the Million Dollar Influencers. Even with the inevitable delays of the US Postal Service[2], you'll get credit in the eyes of the receiver for making an effort.

When meeting a business counterpart at a mutually agreed city to which you each travel, use an excellent facility. Your club membership may have a reciprocal arrangement in the city of the meeting. High-end hotels will reserve meeting rooms and offer extra amenities to make the meeting environment more pleasant, memorable, and productive. When you set the venue, you set the tone.

Travel[3] well, and stop making excuses for not doing so. Taking the redeye on a low-cost carrier may save you $200—but costs you more in wear-and-tear and lost time than you can calculate. Showing up tired and rumpled does not reflect well on you and conveys disrespect for the meeting you're attending. If your travel budget is so tight, should you even be traveling?

Stop wasting time thinking about how to do something instead of just doing it. The pursuit of perfection is masking an underlying fear. Address the fear and press on. Perfection is a myth. We'll discuss needs and wants below, but for now, stop admiring the problem and start doing something to advance your preferred outcome.

Influencers

Perfection is the killer of excellence. You've never experienced a perfect plane flight, dinner, play, book, or athletic event. Why do you expect and seek "perfection" in your decisions and business dealings?

Individually, any of the items above look incredibly easy to implement, and they are. Taken collectively, they will allow you to move faster, making time for more engagements with the right people. The E-Z Pass in your vehicle allows for an individual transaction. When you identify *and use* the other, figurative, E-Z Passes within your reach every day, you'll soon be bypassing traffic in all aspects of your business engagements.

OVERCOMING OBSTACLES

An obstacle isn't necessarily a physical impediment. Obstacles are anything or any condition that inhibits your progress. (Or, you might say, they're what you see when you take your eyes off the goal!) You might not recognize the obstacles around you that can interfere with your exercise of Million Dollar Influence. Obstacles can crop up as "requirements" (either formal or self-imposed) that often have no serious justification for their existence. You can overcome them in four ways: compliance, ignoring them, circumvention, or dismissal.

Process and procedure can appear as obstacles at every turn and can be the quicksand of any business encounter. Bureaucrats thrive in environments steeped in process. Filling out forms, complying with checklists, completing verifications, and conducting due diligence can rob any business arrangement of its energy. Compliance rarely requires imagination or creative thought. Its cousin, conformance, slowly ekes out any initiative.

Case Study: Compliance to process

There is a famous story of an army corporal who served as secretary to a colonel. A messenger arrived with an envelope for the officer, and the corporal entered it into the log and initialed it.

When the colonel returned and was shown the envelope, he told the corporal he was not qualified to initial such a receipt. He then ordered the corporal to erase his initials and initial the erasure.

Process and procedure assure conformance to a minimum standard. Collectively, the rules sustain and standardize operations in mediocrity while stifling creativity. Strive to ignore or circumvent the administrivia of "process." You do this by letting the boss on the other side of the encounter press their version of the command override button. In most major military platforms such as ships, tanks, and aircraft, there are times that require using command override to get through a difficult moment— ignoring procedural compliance for the mission's good.

> **Example:** A jet pilot receives a cockpit alarm of unusual vibration in a single-engine plane. The plane begins losing altitude and the pilot knows they'll need to eject. Left unattended, the engine will automatically shut down and the plane will crash. Observing the civilian homes below, the pilot hits the command override button, allowing the plane to fly further, even outside the engine's normal safe parameters, until it absolutely can't fly further. The pilot's experience allowed them to buy a few more minutes of flight time, saving the lives of civilians below.

Gene works with companies selling to the federal government. Most companies spend far too much time chasing a contract and conforming to the peculiarities of federal contract compliance. They see their primary government point of contact as the contracting official or purchasing agent. *In reality, funding decisions about what capabilities will eventually be acquired occur months and years before a contract official enters the picture.*

Working more carefully with the actual decision-makers about capability and your capacity to deliver will make the contracting process unfold more readily. That's because you can introduce your good ideas further up the chain of command and allow the decision of someone more senior to speed through the bureaucracy for you. Having your idea or solution introduced from the top down will help you circumvent the process at all levels of government: federal, state, and local. You'll have to get a little uncomfortable by working outside your comfort zone at the higher altitudes of an organization.

Learn to identify when compliance is crushing the movement toward your business objectives like a python. Flow charts with yes/no decision points guide the masses to standardized outcomes. It can be helpful for you to understand your counterpart's flowchart to help you both identify opportunities to skip or ignore steps. *While we can all disdain process, the best way to circumvent it is to understand your counterpart's rule book of process.*

Ignoring the rules is always a legitimate option. You can't break the law, but you can bend policy into a horseshoe. Million Dollar Influencers recognize the difference between law and policy. Acts of commission are nearly always forgiven, while acts of omission can signal laziness or sloth. Consciously skipping steps is an act of commission. Working around the other guy's arcane process will speed you to the unconscious competence all Million Dollar Influencers exercise.

Before their first major engagement, nearly all great wartime military leaders develop a deep understanding of their counterpart's doctrine, tactics, and playbook. How much preparation, rehearsal, and general forethought go into your business engagements? We described military training in Chapter 4—it's intense, ongoing, and precedes first contact. Thinking more comprehensively about how you engage a business counterpart can positively change your influence by overcoming obstacles grounded in the process.

> **Example:** Operation Neptune Spear, the CIA-led operation to capture Osama bin Laden in Abbottabad, Pakistan, was preceded by extraordinary levels of preparation. A team from the Joint Special Operations Command worked for months preparing for the actual moment of raid on bin Laden's compound. Scale and actual-size replicas of the compound were constructed in North Carolina and Nevada in advance of the raid. Rehearsals at ground level and at elevation would test the plan's viability. Even with such detailed planning, one helicopter clipped a fence during the raid and had to be destroyed and abandoned. The mission was a success, but did not go exactly as planned. Quick thinking and confidence in their training allowed the team to adapt and proceed, focused on the outcome.

STAYING FOCUSED

You might be the smartest person in the room. *But you might not be.* When you assume you are the smartest person in the room, it can be tempting to spend time conveying extraneous information. "But I want to make sure they understand my context," you say. You may be surprised to learn that you're likely using twice as many words and two-to-three times as much time as necessary. And your audience likely understood you perfectly the first time or is smart enough to ask for clarification. Remember hyper-efficiency with the time identified above? Restating your position multiple times is distracting you and your audience.

Influencers

Tell people what they need to know, not everything that you know.

Let go of the notion that your being right even matters. *It doesn't.* You want to reach preferred outcomes, not get bogged down in redundant exchanges. Focus on the end-game.

Here's an example.

You to the Confidential Assistant:

> I'm calling to get on Secretary Wilson's calendar. We met at the ACME convention on Wednesday, and he agreed we should follow up together directly. He indicated you run the office and handle his schedule.

You're straightforward and responsive to personal interaction with the principal you'd like to meet.

Confidential Assistant: "Secretary Wilson will see you, but new issues need to be run through Assistant Secretary Garfield before we can schedule that meeting."

POTENTIAL DISTRACTION AND DELAY OF GAME

You to the Confidential Assistant:

> I appreciate you have a process that makes sense, so Secretary Wilson doesn't get ambushed by industry. But in this case, since we have begun a dialogue, and he has asked me to follow up directly, I'd hate to see us get wrapped around the process. Would it be possible for Assistant Secretary Garfield to join the meeting? We'll maximize everyone's time and save a meeting altogether.

You acknowledge "the process" but offer a rationale that works for everyone—you keep everyone focused on the outcome.

Jack Nicklaus famously said he never missed a putt. He would execute the stroke as drawn up in his mind, and the ball simply didn't drop. It wasn't a flawed stroke; it was something minor along the line of the putt. This positive mindset would allow him to move on in the round. Such a frame of mind allows the best of the best to see past the small stuff while maintaining focus on the end-game. The Confidential Assistant above is just doing their job. You can help when you're assertive enough to suggest viable alternatives to "process."

Myriad sports stars and coaches have remarked, "We've never lost a game, but we have occasionally run out of time."

"MUSTS" VERSUS "WANTS"

Like the pursuit of perfection, insisting on going for everything on your list in a business encounter is a waste of time. Further, holding out for those additional items of marginal value erodes your credibility. Going into an encounter, you must know what you truly need versus what you can live with as outcomes—identifying the musts before the encounter is essential.

Are you trying to get to the real decision-maker, sell something to meet a specific profit margin, or change an element of legislative tax policy, for example? Each has a different threshold of must versus want. Insisting on getting everything you ask for positions you as an unreasonable negotiator.

It's not that every encounter is a negotiation. Still, use the negotiator's mindset of striving for a range of favorable outcomes instead of a point set of solutions. You'll come away from business encounters much more satisfied. Million Dollar Influencers aren't necessarily going for the gold every time. They seek preferred outcomes that are reasonable in everyone's eyes. The degree of moderation adds to the perception that you're reasonable to deal with, if not downright easy. That means you get to come back and do more or sell more than others.

The traits of a "must" are as follows:

- Absolutely critical to success, can't live without it
- Reasonable and pragmatic to achieve/retain
- Measurable, we know it when we see it

"Wants" are usually "inverted musts." In other words, if the "must" is that something can can's cost more than $50,000, the "want" is that cost is as much below that as possible.

"We must meet no later than the 15th, but if we can meet before that it would be highly desirable."

CHAPTER 8 SUMMARY

Throughout Chapter 8, we identify specific practices *that collectively improve your influence.* When you learn how to incorporate simple habits into your professional style, you'll find that things happen more quickly. They become your "default" setting. When things happen more efficiently, they tend to become more repeatable and their timelines for completion more predictable.

In Chapter 9, we'll learn what the Romans knew about holding things in place as we identify when it's time to "pour some cement."

NOTES

1 The Federal Election Commission (FEC) tracks and reports all federal campaign contributions above $200. www.fec.gov contains a searchable database where anyone can review this information. Campaign contributions are a form of free speech.

2 Some federal government agencies, including Congress, screen mail at an off-site facility for security purposes before ultimate delivery. Allow for this delay which can be several days.

3 The designation of First Class is slowly giving way to the likes of what is actually business class: Polaris (United) or DeltaOne (Delta). The egalitarian identification with an upper class is not the goal—it's the amenities of the higher levels of service that directly contribute to your productivity and wellness!

9

Pouring cement

When applied correctly and in the right conditions, wet cement holds things in place. There comes the point in any business deal when the volleying, jockeying, and positioning for advantage ends. It becomes clear to all parties that alignment with mutual objectives is at hand. Agreement in principle is that sense of recognition that mutual value and remuneration make sense all around.

In some situations, this unfolds relatively quickly, perhaps over a meal. In others, where external entities participate, such as commissions or committees, it may take months. Recognizing this critical moment means it's time to pour cement on the deal. Further discussion will only erode the deal. Pouring cement holds things in place while allowing for a minor adjustment or two before the cement indeed hardens.

THE ART AND SCIENCE OF THE DEAL

We'll use the term "deal" loosely to free your thinking and apply concepts to multiple situations. Although such transactional deals are easiest to recognize, they don't always have to be about a financial exchange for tangible goods. But let's compare the sale of cars with the sale of yachts to see some differences between science and art in a deal. Except for exotic cars, for a long time, when you went to a car dealership in the United States, it was understood that you wouldn't pay the sticker price. A dance unfolded that is both understood and incredibly annoying. *The internet and investigating actual dealer invoicing has largely changed this today, but most of you will recognize this.*

DOI: 10.4324/9781003320388-9

After a test drive, you say to the car salesperson: "*Yes, I think this is the one. How much maneuvering room is there on the price? $60,000 seems higher than I've seen elsewhere. Do you think $50,000 could work?*"

Salesperson: "*Well, I'm not sure. 60 is a very competitive price. Let's write it up, and I can check with my manager. Would you be driving away today if we can make the numbers work?*"

You: "*Yes, I'm prepared to move quickly.*"

Salesperson, after speaking to the manager: "*Great news. I can sell it to you for 5% less at $57,000 out the door.*"

You: "*Hmm. I'll come back. I'd like to do more research at other dealerships. You have my number if something changes.*" You get to your current car only to be stopped by the breathless salesman.

Salesperson after again speaking to the manager: "*I told my manager we can get this done if we meet in the middle at $55,000. How's that? Let's get this done, and you can enjoy this car today.*"

You: "*I can do $55,000 if you'll include the extended warranty and floor mats*" (yes, they still charge extra for floor mats).

This back-and-forth may happen three or four times, nobody walks away feeling totally victorious, and it's petty. Ultimately, you'll get the car, the salesperson gets the minimal commission, and you're happy it's over.

This negative sensation has opened the door to new car buying methods via Carvana or Vroom in the used car market, where there is no haggling and no interaction with a salesperson. Car sales involve a process, but emotion can creep in.

Influencers

While a car purchase is a basic transactional process, it is also the largest single "lifestyle" purchase most people make (people settle on houses but they choose cars). There is a huge emotional component despite the transactional nature—Art and science.

Yacht sales are nuanced, and the buyer's emotion is on full display. It is difficult for boat enthusiasts to contain their likes or dislikes of particular features. The best yacht brokers know how to focus on the experience and lifestyle that the boat and its features will allow. Accurate "comparables" for yacht sales are unavailable to buyers, as they might be in real estate, available only to brokers. Yachts and boats never sell for their list price. The ultimate sales price is often further reduced after a complete boat survey documents its actual mechanical and structural condition.

Gene and his wife, Julie, were "just-looking" to upgrade to a larger yacht. Knowing the brand, we visited the dealer and toured several "brokerage" (not new) boats with an in-house broker. No two boats are exactly alike, nor are how people use boats. Some boats travel extensively; some are "dock queens" that sparkle at the slip but never go anywhere.

Broker: *"Where do you like to cruise? Who travels with you when you go places? What do you like to do en route, and what do you like to do when you get to the destination?"* The questions have little to do with the boat's features or price.

Gene: *"We'd like to take this next one on trips to the Bahamas, pushing out to Exuma, sometimes with family, sometimes alone."* These are details that determine the size and endurance of the best boat for us.

Broker: *"Oh, these are perfect in the Bahamas. Shallow draft, great fuel numbers, comfortable accommodations. You two would have no issue operating this alone or with a couple of grandkids on board."* The focus is on the experience and emotion of time with family in an exotic location, not the price.

Gene: Walking through the pilothouse, *"Looking at the electronics* (chartplotters at multiple stations), *it looks like we'll need to make some upgrades."* Starting to identify costly items for a price reduction.

Broker: *"Well, now you're talking about the cost of replacing a VCR on a million-dollar boat. That's easy stuff. Let's walk through the engine room and see how sturdy and redundant the essential systems are for your and your family's safety. On the way, let's look at where those grandkids might sleep."* Redirecting the conversation, he's now focusing on the family experience.

Yachts are almost never bought after one visit. There are multiple revisits, surveys, and allowances introduced. The seller may find their boat awaiting the right buyer for a year on the market. In yacht sales, there's also a saying, "the first offer by a prospective buyer is almost always the best." Waiting for others to come in and make a more competitive offer doesn't improve the ultimate selling price. Offers on yachts are expressions of emotion.

Influencers

Yacht sales are more art than science. Emotion plays a significant role in the transaction. Price is a secondary factor. A car is required for transportation. A yacht is a luxury for enjoyment.

Whether selling business-to-business, business-to-government, or getting a county commission to approve the construction of a new commercial or residential development, deals in your world often contain elements of both science and art. Process, discussed in previous chapters regarding its ability to inhibit movement, will always be a part of anything, anytime you attempt to influence a preferred outcome. There are rules for any game (game is not meant as a pejorative here). Think of the process and the rules as the science of your engagement. They are inherent, and you'll need to maneuver with them. We talk about moving into an HOV lane in Chapter 8, but you're still taking the highway to your destination. Teleportation isn't here yet! The highway is a metaphor for process.

Science Examples

Requests for proposal
Bid specifications, such as measurements and material requirements
Schedules for delivery
Required votes if dealing with committees or commissions
Audits of finances or capabilities
Required sign-offs or verbal approvals (authorities, in Chapter 2)

The art is more about emotion, as with the yacht sale. The art of engagements exposes the trigger points that help someone change a position, opinion, or finding. As Alan says, "logic makes people think, but emotion moves people to action." For example, changing a tax policy might make a city, county, or state more attractive to businesses or retirees. Taxes might be science, and a means to an end, *but their ramifications are emotional.*

Getting a counterpart to appreciate the better future state your deal supports requires exposing more powerful emotional connections. You may need to help a counterpart see how they might receive the credit when choosing your preferred path. Giving credit away to others can allow them to imagine their improved future states, such as stature, reputation, or even promotion.

It's amazing what you can accomplish if you do not care who gets the credit.

— Harry S. Truman

The COVID-19 pandemic provided an opening for people of all walks to evaluate their situation. "Is this job experience what I want for my life?" "Does the company need this office and meeting space?" "Do we need a brick-and-mortar presence in Times Square?" The *emotions* of the pandemic exposed opportunities to change the science of some arrangements not seriously considered previously. Million Dollar Influencers recognize these conditions for an emotional response without needing a pandemic as a backdrop!

Art Examples

Higher employee morale
Enhanced reputation of the counterpart
The improved reputation of a company or entity
Potential promotion or increased authority of the counterpart
Recognition in all forms
Improved quality of life or work circumstances

Companies thriving during the pandemic, despite the challenging circumstances, were those driven to act. Generac, a provider of back-up power generators, continues to capitalize on energy in transition and was not thwarted by the pandemic. Bath & Body Works, a presence in many malls, capitalized on the online experience with $2 billion in revenue through e-commerce. Etsy recognized masks and home décor would surge during the pandemic and rode the wave connecting buyers and sellers. Ten percent of Etsy's 2020 revenue came from mask sales. Enphase Energy, a provider of energy storage and associated software was also undeterred. The stock value of each rose more than 200%. That's not luck—that's being prepared to capitalize.

Business winners were those prepared for the storm with cash and flexible internal policies, and those who recognized the rapidly changing circumstances. More importantly, *overcoming the emotion of fear* to adapt, innovate, and succeed can separate multiple winners from those that succumb to their circumstances.

During a significant chip shortage attributed to pandemic-induced supply chain issues and faced with the prospect of not completing their new cars to the original specifications, Tesla figured out how to reprogram the software in their cars to use the different available chips. How's that for "improv" (Chapter 4)—Elon Musk accepted what was given and influenced sales where others languished. Science and emotion are both evident here.

DEMONSTRATING JOINT "WINS"

There shouldn't be losers when speaking of influence. In the car dealership, it can feel like win/lose, which is part of the experience's negative sensation. The dealerships want the most margin possible on every deal. They set the high point of the negotiation with the price. The setting of the low point is up to the buyer, who is not nearly as skilled in negotiating. (Most car buyers are afraid to set the lowest low point out of embarrassment.) It's uncommon for people to walk away from a car purchase feeling like they've won on price. Despite having the car they want, they might feel they lost by leaving more money at the dealership than intended.

Million Dollar Influencers try and identify multiple ways both sides of a business deal can feel great about an outcome. That means looking for opportunities throughout your engagement and relationship to reinforce value for the other guy. This awareness of opportunities applies to engagements with business and government alike. Remember meeting the other guy 60/40 in Chapter 6? When you leave something on the table, and the other person perceives value for who or what they represent, there are multiple winners.

Influencers

We tell our entrepreneurial clients that "win/win" is possible and desirable. The client believes high value was received, and the entrepreneur believes the fee paid was equitable and fulfilling.

In a competition where your company competes directly against others for the business, the other competitors won't feel like winners. It's the decider you are looking out for here, not your competitor. So, let's not confuse the concept of multiple winners (you and your counterpart) with you courteously standing to "hold the door," so to speak, for everyone else. You want to present yourself and your offering across four factors that establish you as the most rational, logical, price-sensitive, implementable, and agreeable "best value" compared to all others. The cumulative effects separate you from the competition when you make such an effort.

In business, the word value can be synonymous with "win." Where you can demonstrate value, you're identifying how participants in the deal will win. Demonstrating value is another way to ease points of friction and lower barriers to moving forward in any deal. Let's look at ways to show value in each of the four factors from above.

Rational/Logical: Common sense and facts
- Eight out of ten experts in the relevant ecosystem would agree what you're proposing makes perfect sense
- You may be the only one to suggest your particular solution because others didn't think of it or couldn't articulate it
- Your proposal improves the condition of your counterpart
- You specifically address the incorporation of risk mitigation
- Your proposal addresses known and identifiable concerns with acceptable solutions
- You address the identifiable technical specifications, even if they are not entirely solved. If a specification is not yet solvable, you allow for how it might be achievable in the future

Price-Sensitive: Not the same as cheapest
- Lowest cost to the buyer over time, not necessarily at the point of sale
- Best value to the buyer, suggesting your solution will be lasting, won't require rework, and is confirmed "once and done"
- Discount based on order quantity, payment terms, or attractive credit terms
- Open to a lease or lease-to-buy option
- The quality of the proposed solution warrants a higher price, such as the use of unique or highly specialized materials, extraordinary craftsmanship, or premium brand association

- No "tail" of follow-on or sustainment costs buried in the deal
- Sometimes a policy change will remove or mitigate a business obstacle

Implementable: You know how to get it done
- Ready to begin immediately or on an agreeable fixed date
- Able to prioritize this opportunity above others in the distribution of your work force
- Required training is built into the deal
- No additional costs are masked, such as a requirement for additional hires or management structures
- The first steps and end-state are within sight and reach

Agreeable: You're the person who understands your counterpart
- You demonstrate with your words and actions that you understand and respect your counterpart's chosen path
  - *"We understand your preference for incorporating recyclable materials where possible."*
  - *"You've indicated a desire to complete within six months, and our schedule for start and implementation is equally aggressive."*
- You recognize *and convey* that there will nearly always be more than one "right" answer
  - *"That can also work."*
- You don't "die on a hill" holding out for your counterpart to agree to every point in your proposal, and you are open to adjusting your proposal or offering
  - *"We can set that element aside for now and decide later if we need to revisit."*

TRANSITIONING TO IMPLEMENTATION

When the sommelier brings you a wine list, they don't rush to blurt out everything they know about wine. They may ask questions about your preferences, what you might choose as an entrée or if you have a prior favorite type of wine. You may ask some questions of the sommelier about pairings or labels. It's a gentle back-and-forth focused on getting a wine that you and your guests will enjoy with your meal. (If you choose a wine yourself, the sommelier will almost always say, "Excellent choice," even if it's the Ripple from this past May. "But better than April, sir.")

When the sommelier returns with your wine, a sequence unfolds. Confirmation of the label, carefully removing the seal, skillfully removing the cork, allowing you to taste a sample, gaining your approval, then meticulously filling glasses at the table. Notice the label can be seen by anyone looking, even from another table (selling others). The sommelier may respond to questions, but it's about delivering the experience once you make your selection. The best sommeliers know when to stop selling.

Million Dollar Influencers don't fill every moment with words. During any exchange, there are times when it's ok to let your counterpart think and absorb your suggestion, idea, or proposal. In considering the four factors above, a sense should emerge that what you're presenting resonates. Your use of language has positioned you well, and you should be picking up on signals and indications that you're in general agreement, if not complete agreement, with your proposal.

The car dealer above may start to sweat at this stage because the window of opportunity is so narrow in a typical car deal. A fickle buyer may walk away or otherwise grandstand out of nervousness that they may be overextending themselves on price. (Don't forget that car dealerships are usually "bunched" together like cans on a shelf making it easy to walk over to the competition.) The yacht broker recognizes that the buyer may not commit today with an offer, but the emotional connection with the yacht is usually clear. The offer on a yacht can be implemented over the phone or by email, and it's not critical that the keys are transferred at the point of agreement to proceed. The latter concept applies in Million Dollar Influence.

Moving toward implementing any deal is about confirming what Alan identifies as "conceptual agreement." The four factors above allow both sides to recognize that they are on the same page, their objectives align, and it makes sense to move forward. Emphasizing what should be clear, this conceptual agreement applies to any business-to-business or business-to-government arrangement. It could be as diverse as a direct sale of a tangible item, pursuing a policy change, an agreement to partner, or a funding request.

The cement truck is now in position. It's for you to put the cement chute in place and open the valve allowing wet cement to pour onto the arrangement. Examples of words that confer conceptual agreement and begin the flow of cement include the following:

Would you agree we seem to have a framework before us that works for us?

If we can transpose our conversation(s) about the relevant points to a contract, it looks like we're ready to proceed.

Are there others we need to inform that we've reached this level of agreement?

I like your solution(s), and think we can proceed as soon as we take this to the committee for final endorsement.

Let's summarize the high points and move from the rough order of magnitude pricing to a definitized price as soon as we can.

Can we shake on this and agree to move forward? We can tidy up the details with the standard contract.

Actual implementation requires that you make the next steps crystal clear for your counterpart. While you may be responsive to the specifics of the verbal exchange, you will have prepared for this moment and know where you are trying to go. Your thorough understanding of their hierarchy, flow (process and content), and decision authorities allows you to drive the conversation confidently.

Influencers

You understand precisely where you are in the organization and know that the right person understands your position.

The next steps have both a time and a place associated with them. You may even have a flow sheet or index card at the ready that allows your counterpart to see the implementation framework on paper. The following are examples that weave in a*ction, time, and place,* without sounding desperate for the close:

Bill, the committee meets in ten days. What if my team and I helped develop your presentation of our idea this week? We've got 99% of it complete from our discussions to date. Would that work for you?

Jan, committing the subcontractors to meet the timeline we've discussed will require minor deposits. I can invoice those first steps immediately, and we can lock in the schedule. Shall I send that directly to you, or is there a finance lead or comptroller I can meet?

Jennifer, in other successful deals like this, there is generally a Memorandum of Agreement. Do you have a standard MOA, or may I provide one? I'm authorized to lock this in today.

Dan, the policy change can be implemented with a few paragraphs under agency letterhead. Can we convert what we've agreed into an agency policy memo? That could be communicated within the week or at the outside or outside this month. How can I help with that process?

Your body language doesn't convey you "need" this agreement at this moment. *It can't.* You must maintain a matter-of-fact demeanor as you outline the way forward. You are transitioning from a peer to a guide in the eyes of your counterpart. The odds are your counterpart hasn't thought this through as well as you have before coming together for your meeting(s). *The fact is, you've been the guide all along because you are driving the conversation.*

Think about it; you have an idea or concept. You master your counterpart's organization and know the terrain probably much better than your counterpart knows you. You are outlining a logical proposal that addresses a need of some type. Your measured approach is considerate of legitimate concerns and, as you are now demonstrating, is readily implementable.

Ideally, you are positioning your counterpart and the organization to be in a better condition! You may be controlling the cement truck right now, but you've been moving through the HOV lane with the skill of the racecar driver (Chapter 8). You are exercising Million Dollar Influence.

When the guest in the weekend foursome in front of you hollers in delight that a three-foot putt was made for birdie, it's embarrassing to the regular golfers. Act like you've been there before!

DISENGAGING

When a relative visits family, the trip can end with what amounts to a long goodbye in some cultures. Kisses, hugs, tears, and more hugs precede the eventual departure of the relative. You see it regularly in airports and train stations. Family members may make a considerable sacrifice to travel some distance just to be with their relatives. It's touching to observe. *But long goodbyes are for family, not for Million Dollar Influencers.*

You don't want to be the guest who wouldn't leave or simply couldn't read the room to recognize the meeting is over! If you enter an engagement with a preferred outcome in mind, you either get to that outcome, or you don't. You must know when and how to depart.

Influencers

Depart with the other party looking forward to meeting again, not trying to figure out how to get rid of you. Always leave people wanting more.

Gene's eight-minute rule of messaging (SM) (Chapter 3) focuses the meeting on the fast delivery of relevant information and giving time back to your counterpart. As you move toward implementation, it's no longer about delivering your message with extreme efficiency. Now it's about an orderly transition, which means your presence may no longer be required. When the next steps are in place, there needs to be a handoff to a plan of execution.

You to your counterpart:

> Mr. Mayor, the language of the amendment aligns with your public position and will allow for timely reconfiguration and development of the land. We can execute the plan immediately after the commission vote next week. Why don't we have our project manager pencil in the start dates with the City Manager and let them take it from there?

You to your business counterpart:

> Larry, just to clarify what the order of operations looks like from my perspective, we begin phase 1 in March, phase 2 in June and we're complete by August. Why don't we move this over to the contracts team and you and I can get out of the way?

You to your representative:

Congressman, with the markup just two weeks out, it was important for us to check in and make sure we haven't left any questions unanswered. Thank you for your support of ACME, the employees and their families. We can't ask for more than that.

In each case, you're controlling the dialogue, confirming the agreement, clarifying dates, and setting conditions for others to take over. Importantly, the language is not heavy-handed or desperate. You understand how things work and you speak in a manner that conveys expertise and credibility.

Depending on the agreed arrangement, there might be a project manager, program manager, assistant secretary, or other relevant executive overseeing progress. Identifying those accountabilities is critical to your disengagement and a successful handoff. For example, there may be specific steps involved in finalizing a plan, whether it's an acquisition contract, confirmation of policy language, or transfer of control of material and equipment.

As the guide in the relationship, the Million Dollar Influencer steers the counterpart to those steps or clarifies those accountabilities. The cement is beginning to harden the arrangements you've choreographed. This is not the time to introduce or allow any game delays (Chapter 6). You reach a conceptual agreement, identify the next steps of implementation, prepare for a handoff by clarifying accountabilities, *and leave.*

There is no long goodbye and no extended celebration. Doing so changes the dynamic and is no longer moving your relationship forward. Save the emotion for the time in the future when you can rekindle and work together on your next mutual engagement.

CHAPTER 9 SUMMARY

Chapter 9 focuses on recognizing when you are close to closing in on the conceptual agreement, holding things in place with some binding cement, and transitioning to logical next steps. Suggesting some phrases to use while reinforcing concepts that help move you along, you see how Million Dollar Influence conveys confidence through words and actions. That confidence helps others feel great about following your lead.

In Chapter 10, we'll address how you build on the single engagement and develop a pattern of success. Million Dollar Influencers might occasionally score quick wins, but your real influence accumulates over time and through your ability to replicate the success over and over.

10

Capitalizing on success

Quick wins are for amateurs and (lucky) start-ups. When starting from a position with no cash flow, the pressure on a start-up to close a quick deal may be intense. Closing the quick win may mean the difference between making payroll or not. However, Million Dollar Influence is about setting conditions for sustained wins that will unfold repeatedly.

Throughout the book, we have identified the countless ways to apply influence to advance any situation. When properly applied, your exercise of influence will move you to a position of respect and credibility. People will seek you out to work with you. Consistent performance and delivery of your word will fuel long-lasting and positive business relationships.

Million Dollar Influence is a perpetual process.

EXTENDING RELATIONSHIPS

Navy ships at sea prepare for warfare in three dimensions. A simple mnemonic device, "Up, Down, and Out," captures the three-dimensional nature of warfare at sea. The air threat (the up) can be a simple hand-held drone or a sophisticated hypersonic missile that descends vertically or near sea level, just feet off the water.

The submarine threat (the down) is obvious, anything beneath the water's surface, manned or autonomous. The surface threat (the out) comes from enemy ships that can launch missiles or fire guns at a great distance. Maintaining vigilance in three dimensions saves missions and lives.

DOI: 10.4324/9781003320388-10

Thinking up, down, and out in business can create opportunities not visible when you first approach a counterpart's organization. This perspective is a mindset you can ingrain.

Influencers

As we are writing this book, a technologically inferior Ukrainian force was able to strike the Russian flagship of the Black Sea fleet. A poor defensive posture left the flagship vulnerable. While retreating to sea, the flagship sunk, at least partly due to poor training in damage control responses. They lost focus on "up, down, and out." Companies suffer the same fate. Again, as we write this, Netflix stock has lost about 30% of its worth because subscribers have shared passwords with non-subscribers globally.

While your engagement with any counterpart won't feel like open-ocean warfare, the metaphor applies to how you engage your counterpart's business or agency. Before your first contact, you should be thinking about who else you should be in contact with and who should be aware of the preferred outcome you aim to achieve.

In government, officials rotate regularly. Elected officials lose elections, die in office, or otherwise leave office (as in "scandal"). In business, teams are in continuous motion, with players moving in and out of roles. You don't want complete reliance on a single line of connection that puts your initiative at risk of a single-point failure.

It's appropriate for you to do your homework before going into an organization, as we discuss thoroughly in Chapter 2. Once you are in, it's also appropriate, even vital, for you to seek additional introductions "up, down, and out." In some cases, you won't even need to ask for the introduction because other influencers and enablers will be part of the process flow. Pay attention to who these people are—today's influencers and enablers are tomorrow's decision-makers.

Even company presidents respond to an "up" in the form of a board. Don't dismiss the possibility that you can interact with board members. Remember those professional clubs suggested in Chapter 8? When we say "interact with board members," that means light-touch conversations, *not* you independently taking the same issue over the head of your primary contact to a board member. The emphasis here is on remaining alert for the opportunities to attach like Velcro to your counterpart's organization "up, down, and out." If your counterpart leaves, you'll have other contacts in place. Following are some soft-touch examples.

You in a group setting:

> It's great to meet the others working with Bob on this land-use arrangement. Aside from those at the table, are there others who will participate in the process which I should know or be introduced?

You to a principal counterpart:

> Leslie, I think we're getting close to alignment of our mutual objectives. I notice Tim Murray is the subcommittee lead for the board on such deals. Is there an appropriate time we might brief Tim together before this is addressed publicly?

You to a counterpart in an agency:

> With the change of administration, is there a transition team that should be aware of this arrangement? Or are there people you expect to rotate out over the coming months? I'd be happy to help bring others up to speed with you.

You to an agency acquisition executive:

> Do you have a contracting team you work with routinely? Could we find a time to introduce me to that part of your process so I'm not bothering you once we get to the final execution details?

Influence

It's not uncommon for the receptionist of a congressional office to have a Master's Degree and have taken the position to get a foot in the door. Within a couple of years, that same receptionist may be a senior policy advisor or professional staff member of a committee with influence over your issue.

We discussed your digital identity in Chapter 5. Love it or hate it, LinkedIn has evolved into a vast repository of professional information. Social media channels will continue to evolve, and some will genuinely be flashes in the pan—remember Clubhouse and Periscope? LinkedIn was once a platform where people loosely browsed for jobs and passively signaled a desire to change positions.

Today's LinkedIn is an efficient way to fill seams in your knowledge of an organization and your Rolodex. The Sales Navigator features allow you to target and identify companies, agencies, and individuals by name, job title, and time in the role by capitalizing on advances in artificial intelligence. These features will strengthen your research allowing you to harvest valuable personnel data with low labor. This supplemental information has value and is much less costly or time-consuming than attending trade shows hoping to gather contacts. Use these tools after identifying some of these additional up, down, and out relationships you'd like to strengthen.

Your goal is to extend your principal relationship and spider-web your way through an organization. Further, and more importantly, this collective knowledge will contribute to your extending the length of time that you're able to maintain a positive relationship with a counterpart's organization. Salespeople strive to "make a number," thereby focusing on the wrong thing, missing this critical factor. You want to be able to come back for a long time into the future, not just complete the present deal.

While the immediate quarterly sales target matters, it's the understanding of the "up, down, and out" nature of the other relationships that will allow your relationship with the organization to have more *depth, substance, and endurance.* With enduring relationships in place, the follow-on engagements become easier to influence, opportunities materialize more readily, and you'll find you are sought after for your trustworthy counsel by leaders and future leaders. You'll simply be a known commodity by more people you may work with in the future.

Examples of companies where up, down, and out thinking is evident include the following:

SpaceX's Starlink[1] internet aimed at underserved portions of the world with lower cost, distributable systems for internet connectivity.

Salesforce now offers much more than its well-known Customer Relationship Management (CRM) tools. Through acquisition and strategic investments, they are a cloud computing company serving adjacencies up, down, and out with products across industries.

Keurig Dr. Pepper (KDP), recognizing changes in soft drink habits, is methodically disrupting the global market dominance of Coke and Pepsi by merging the hot and cold drink markets.[2]

Note: The point is not that you need to be a multi-billion-dollar company to exert influence, but you can learn from them by observing how they maneuver up, down, and out.

Knowing these people can give you multiple reasons to reengage down the road. Examples of your rekindling a connection based on knowing something or working with someone in another capacity previously include the following:

Tom, I remember us working through the tax implications of HR 1234 two years ago. Nice to see you in the new role. I'd like to come to visit to discuss a similar concept to see if we can try that path on another issue. I think we can get you an early win on this. Do you have some time in your calendar next week?

Mary, good to see you at the Nats game last week. It's amazing how this team has ridden the wave. Seeing you reminded me, I'd like to drop in and discuss a pressing issue very similar to the ACME deal we worked on last year. Can we grab 15 minutes over coffee to discuss later this week?

Sandra, it seems like yesterday I was asking for time with the boss, and you were always so gracious in helping me get in. It's great to see you now serving on the committee; everyone knew it was only a matter of time. I know you'll find it interesting in this role, an issue that I would like to share. Can we schedule a few minutes for me to stop by, or would you have a couple of minutes now where I give you the high points?

In each case, you ground the prior connection and the success you both were a part of. Your request is to reconnect, and you are not asking for a lot of time. Your follow-up must be with that soft touch. In a culture where spending hours per week watching streaming services[3] or sitting through back-to-back meetings[4] are the norm, who can't spare a few minutes for somebody they have previously enjoyed success with?

An additional benefit of knowing even more people in organizations you interact with is the opportunity to grow your base of referrals exponentially. The business will be referred to you when you are successful. Even more, you will feel completely confident *asking* more people for referrals.

People want to talk about their success with others and are always willing to share a story of success of which you might have been a critical part.

DEMONSTRATING SUCCESS

In government, prior successful performance matters so much that it carries specific weight in evaluating vendors in subsequent competitions. A standard grade is assigned to technical quality, timeliness of performance, cost control, management performance, and small business use. The Contractor Performance Assessment Reporting System (CPARS) uses subjective grading such as "exceptional," "very good," "satisfactory," "marginal," and "unsatisfactory." In this scale, "satisfactory" or below doesn't keep you in the game very long. CPARS is simplified even further with corresponding color codes, blue for best and red for worst, of performance. Blue and red scores both jump off the page—make blue your favorite color! Consistently playing toward the test and knowing how competitions are evaluated matters.

Influencers

You don't want this to be a figure skating contest, where the US judge gives you a 9.5 but the Romanian judge gives you a 2.3 since a countryman is also competing!

In business relationships, sometimes similar measuring scales are used to evaluate performance. Manufacturing, production schedules, and supply chain performance are data-driven and lend well to such measurement. However, in business, a positive reputation can often play an even more significant role than in government and can trump metrics. Reputation is a direct function of your credibility and integrity and can help overcome the inevitable error, mistake, or shortcoming that might not have been within your control.

Million Dollar Influencers measure their success and that of their relationships through adherence to a simple mantra: *Do what you say you will do.* This straightforward phrase focuses any engagement on what matters—are you capable of getting it done? When you say, you'll have the draft ready for review on Thursday, make it happen by Thursday or sooner.

Credibility is lost in the smallest of increments over time; protect yours by overdelivering whenever you can.

To overdeliver, you can't overpromise, ever. It can be tempting to overstate your capability or capacity. Don't risk it. Maintaining your credibility requires specific knowledge of the work you are influencing. It requires your attention to specific relevant attributes such as the improvement of a condition, timeliness, cost estimation and control, performance of a technology or system, and the dozens of things that add up to your solution being viable.

Collectively these credibility attributes represent the integrity of your Million Dollar Influence in the form of successes.

Examples of overpromising include the following:

- Autonomous cars and trucks will dominate the interstate
  - *Autonomy is coming for a segment of these vehicle markets, but the cost of the technology and the size of the used car market suggest we are many years from autonomy dominating either*
- Drones will deliver packages to your doorstep within ten years
  - *First claimed in 2013 by Jeff Bezos*
- If you can accelerate funding, we can build out within months
  - *Vague and applies pressure as opposed to influencing; you want the mutual and achievable win*

FedEx ran ads in the late 1970s "When it absolutely, positively has to be there overnight." The campaign helped fuel the company's growth to become the largest express shipping company globally. If you can deliver on the iron-clad guarantee ("absolutely, positively"), then you are not overpromising. But are you as good as FedEx?

Influencers

American Express famously proclaimed "Don't leave home without it." But along came the pandemic, and no one was leaving home!

Amex changed the expectations by altering the phrase to, "Don't live life without it!"

Brilliant.

You erode your credibility if you promise the moon and deliver a streetlight. When you frame outcomes, you anticipate realistic, achievable, and mutually agreeable terms for your counterpart based on your knowledge of the facts and landscape. Doing so, you improve the likelihood of delivering success.

Examples of where and how success can be demonstrated before, during, and after an engagement you seek to influence include the following:

- Pricing based on markets, futures, economic order quantities, or efficiencies
  - *Irrefutable facts support the successful outcome, such as inflation will rise when the government prints and distributes money to offset economic hardship*
- Morale of an organization as measured by retention, sick days, or wellness surveys
  - *Metrics of workforce health reflect further savings beyond the success of the initial outcome, and how often employees recommend new hires is a sign of a healthy workforce*
- Improvements in sales, revenues, profits, retention, delivery times, overhead costs, or production quantities
  - *Measuring business health brings clarity to the work; allows for the evaluation of predictions and outcomes, and also includes qualitative measures, such as unsolicited client referrals*
- Incorporation of your preferred wording or objectives in agency policy, committee proclamations, budgets, or legislation
  - *Proof in the finalized document*
- Modeling your proposal for future outcomes using examples where others improved in similar situations
  - *You help your counterpart see their future through the prior performance of others*
- You introduce new partners or teaming opportunities to your counterpart
  - *Exercising your network for the benefit of others and eventually receiving reciprocal value*
- You take control of an engagement by driving the meeting schedules, overseeing arrangements, and taking what mundane burdens from your counterpart that you can

- *This doesn't mean you do all the work, but you roll up your sleeves and participate in developing inertia, contributing to your positive reputation as someone who is accountable*

You demonstrate success throughout Million Dollar Influence. It's not a near-term objective; it's an overarching mindset. Say what you can do, do it, then review the facts of what you accomplished together.

RINSE, REPEAT, THEN DO IT AGAIN

The business cycle is taught early in business and management curricula. The balance of gross domestic product (GDP) and employment reveals identifiable peaks and troughs following periods of growth and recession, respectively. Over time, GDP generally trends upward, but occasional fluctuations can cause downdrafts for those not attuned to the business environment.

The business cycle is knowable, but too many people ignore the signs of trouble or don't take adequate precautions in changing markets. Even the "best companies" can fall. General Electric will be a case study for years to come for failing to adapt GE Capital, one portion of the overall business, under the leadership of Jeff Immelt.

General Electric misread the clear signals to reconfigure the conglomerate during one of the most extended and most significant economic booms. It lost over 500 billion dollars in market cap in a few years. In 2018, GE was removed from the Dow Jones Industrial Average. Where was the governance of the board of directors? Some say corporate hubris got in the way. Ultimately, GE failed to recognize the visible signs of regular business cycles.

It is now in three separate parts and still saddled with billions in debt.

Budgets also execute in cycles, often of one- or two-years' duration. The US federal budget is funded annually, although the budget process takes three years to complete in most agencies. Yes, it takes three years for a single fiscal year's budget to be approved. In state and local governments, most budgets are approved and funded annually (and in many cases, money is spent wildly at the conclusion of the year because unused funds are often taken back and next year's allocation will reflect that lower need).

Policy reviews at federal, state, and local levels are in perpetual motion and can be addressed at almost any time. *Since policy is not law, it can be influenced more quickly than a budget* through several means such as executive orders, amendments, interim policy changes, or memoranda. Policy changes can often change the competitive landscape.

Case Study: The magnets

Gene works with a magnet manufacturer reliant on specialized materials only available off-shore. Congress took a strong stand and declared that the specialized materials would only be allowed from US or allied nation sources. This well-intended legislation would also stop the US magnet business, and delay programs as re-qualification of new supply chains would take years.

Gene and the company president met with congressional and agency decision-makers explaining the negative short-term impact, despite the legislation's good intent. A change in both law and policy restored the prior supply chain on an interim basis, allowing business to flow while supply chains had time to adjust.

You don't have to run a large company, or run any company, to exert Million Dollar Influence. But you have to recognize the opportunities in your environment. The cyclic nature of business, legislation, and policy review offers multiple opportunities across a broad playing field where you can engage at the right place and time.

Million Dollar Influence is a long game; not one played over months or quarters. When you are successfully influencing an outcome that improves your counterpart or client's condition, you feel great and want to repeat it. But repeating the success in the same manner with the same counterpart may not be possible in the near term. That's okay, and you don't need to force a replay.

By understanding cycles, you can look for scenarios that may allow multiple opportunities to play out on staggered timelines, sometimes over multiple years. Occasionally, you'll notice a situation while working on one project with a counterpart where you can suggest an additional solution set. The stage for a replay of your success can be set while you're still working on the first project.

MAKING THE NEXT ONE BETTER

Along the way to your understanding of your counterpart, they recognize you as a credible guide true to your word, highly competent, and worthy of their trust. Showing up well-prepared, well-informed, at the right place and time, and communicating a time-sensitive message with a viable, appropriate, mutually agreeable outcome all add up. These collective actions distinguish you from a sea of empty suits and *poseurs*. Most people will not put in the work we've discussed in the previous chapters.

"I don't have time for all that research. I've got to get my proposal formatted for submission" is the equivalent of not obeying traffic signals. It will lead to a crash. Your competitors in most endeavors behave in this manner, letting their short attention span and lack of focus on objectives force them through a do loop of failure work. They'll wonder how you continue to make it look so easy.

Much of your initial effort in getting to know your counterpart's organization will pay dividends helping you overdeliver the next time. Your knowledge of relationships, authorities, accountabilities, and responsibilities from your deliberate effort stays with you. Ideally, you don't simply load it all into a company's CRM tool that you don't own and can't take with you. This is your influence we're talking about! Keep the information you've worked so hard to collect. We've identified ways you piece actionable intelligence together to know *and understand* your counterpart throughout the book.

You'll find that when you've achieved initial success using the methods we outline throughout, *the subsequent engagements can move more quickly and with even less effort on your part*. Your energy is free to be even more creative or attentive to the marginal activities. You can more readily recognize special occasions like birthdays or weddings and grab a meal or coffee without a work-related agenda.

When you begin staggering your engagements across multiple counterparts, the abundance stemming from your work relieves what may have been pressure to perform. Your confidence will be on full display, and your counterparts will notice—so will everyone else. As the saying goes, nothing succeeds like success[5].

But coasting isn't a part of Million Dollar Influence. As Alan identifies, coasting only works because the "coaster" is going downhill. You'll need to continue to grow and evolve. While we use the phrase "rinse and repeat" above, that doesn't mean running the same play repeatedly. If that were effective, we'd still get movies at Blockbuster, order from the Sears catalog, or ask secretaries to bring coffee into a meeting! Evolving requires that you continue to be informed and educate yourself.

Unfortunately, in both government and business, it's uncommon for individuals to participate in a serious effort to continue education. They'll do the required minimum so long as the company or the agency pays for it. But too few invest their own money in truly improving themselves professionally. Million Dollar Influencers tune into growth opportunities and schedule them into their routine.

You don't have to complete additional university-level education to evolve. But you have to keep up. Twenty-three percent of Americans did not read a book in whole or in part, in any form[6] in 2021. This trend is worsening, and it fuels more opportunities. Did your parents scoff at online shopping, cameras in phones, or not carrying cash? Think about technological changes of the past ten years alone and then close your eyes and try to imagine what's next.

Influencers

Alan has written over 60 books for eight publishers appearing in 15 languages. He disembarked from a long trip to Australia and announced that the flight was great, he finished an entire book.

His client asked, "Do you mean you read one or wrote one?"

Engaging your imagination to envision the future is a difficult task and one that is readily avoided by most. You'll find your counterparts are most comfortable engaging their memory to think about the past, "how we've always done it." Others have paralysis due to the present challenge; they perceive an immediate problem because they can't see an alternative. Million Dollar Influencers know about and can see the alternatives more clearly because they keep up with trends.

Significant change does not come about with a big bang; change evolves. Look at the internet and its relatively short lifespan.[7] Today's internet is nothing close to what the Advanced Research Project Agency (ARPA) network spawned as the first such "net" in the 1960s. Think about what was the information age (Internet 1.0 of the 1980s–1990s), cloud-based computing where we no longer need large processors in our building (Internet 2.0 of the 2000s), and the emerging methods of machine learning and artificial intelligence (Internet 3.0 underway).

Similarly, we won't just jump to blockchain technology to make a frictionless business transaction or infrastructure to support cars' full electrification or technology's implantation in humans to ease suffering and extend life. All of these things are happening now, but not at scale. Most have only a passing awareness of any of them. There are so many ways the world is evolving, and most are along for the ride, not paying attention. Close your eyes and name two trends you've observed in the past year. The Million Dollar Influencers are not just along for the ride; they ask questions like this of themselves.

Information, education, and knowledge are essential ingredients that will allow you to make the next one better. The real key is that Million Dollar Influencers are highly aware of their environment, paying close attention to people, conditions, trends, tone, leadership changes, technology applications, and most importantly, alignment of objectives.

Million Dollar Influence is available to anyone willing to make an effort. How will you make that effort and exercise your Million Dollar Influence?

CHAPTER 10 SUMMARY

In Chapter 10, we acknowledge that the action and requirements of Million Dollar Influence are within your reach. Your demonstration of its applications in your world, even just one time, means you can "rinse and repeat" and "do it even better." The Million Dollar Influencer, who appears to move with such ease through business situations, is working a lot harder than they let on.

It's not easy to exercise Million Dollar Influence, but it is within your reach. Million Dollar Influence gets easier to apply when your success and reputation now generate *equity that speaks for you* even when you're not in the room!

We wish you Million Dollar success!

NOTES

1 Starlink was able to rapidly deploy to Ukraine in 2022 when war-related physical and cyber damage took down traditional internet services. Awareness of the environment allowed Starlink to readily fill a critical need on short notice.

2 Fortune reports 30% of the more than $1 billion dollar market growth during the pandemic went to KDP. See https://fortune.com/2020/10/19/keurig-growth-coffee-dr-pepper-ai-beverage-industry/

3 Americans spend nearly twelve hours per day connected to a media device (phone, television, computer), and streaming times are increasing nearly 20% annually. See https://datareportal.com/reports/digital-2022-global-overview-report?utm_source=Global_Digital_Reports&utm_medium=Article&utm_campaign=Digital_2022

4 MIT's Sloan Management Review identifies executives spend 23 hours per week in meetings! See www.inc.com/geoffrey-james/you-simply-wont-believe-how-much-time-you-waste-in-meetings-at-work-according-to-mit.html

5 The idiom is attributed by some to the French Bishop Autun, appearing in *The Baptist Magazine* in 1859.

6 According to Pew Research. See www.pewresearch.org

7 And we'll remind you that while human kind has been around for perhaps 10,000 years or so, the dinosaurs ruled for 129 *million years*, and the iconic Tyrannosaurus Rex lived closer to our age than to that of the earliest dinosaurs preceding him.

Index

Pages in *italics* refers figures and pages followed by n refers notes.

Printed in the United States
by Baker & Taylor Publisher Services

Printed in the United States
by Baker & Taylor Publisher Services